CONTENTS

PREFACE

My husband always said I was a tortured soul - always worrying and overthinking. So a few years ago, in order to calm my chattering mind, balance the daily stress of life and ultimately find peace and happiness, I turned back to my Buddhist roots and began to practice it in earnest.

The real challenge came about when I tried to explain some of these teachings to my daughter. How do you explain to a nine-year-old why you shouldn't hit back when someone hits you? That it doesn't matter if you're not as pretty, or smart or popular as your friends? How do you handle the fear of failure? Of jealousy? How do you train focus and what is mindfulness? How could I share these teachings with a young person in a way that could be understood?

Both of us being equally hot-tempered, I found that the best way to impart any sort of advice was not to do so - not directly anyway and certainly not in the heat of the moment as emotions would run high, arguments would invariably ensue, and neither she nor I would be really listening to the other. So it was by accident really that I wrote the first story - Oww That Hurt - which in effect illustrates the laws of causality (karma) and left that lying around for her to read.

There are many books out there on Buddhist teachings but nothing I could find that was relatable to what we encounter today that children can identify with, understand and apply. I needed something in between the heavy philosophical texts and the traditional stories. So the story grew into a storybook - set in a typical London suburb, about a typical schoolgirl and the typical challenges she and her peers face. Through these, the Four Noble Truths that encapsulate the basics of Buddhist teachings are brought to life, explained in parts through the character of Uncle, created in memory of my father (and yes, I can tell you those teeth were no exaggeration!)

Then of course this book touches upon the subject of death which, even in this day and age, is still taboo. Growing up in Southeast Asia opposite a cemetery, a sizeable part of my childhood was spent watching, with great interest, the lively processions of funerals pass by the house: colourful caskets, deafening drums, clashing cymbals followed by trails and trails of mourners bawling with gusto. Death is something that needs to be acknowledged more and it takes time, a lifetime perhaps, to get round mentally. I feel that training our minds to view and handle this ultimate nature of reality from a younger age is essential - it is one of the things that forms part of a lifelong journey of learning and training of the mind for every Buddhist - and it takes time, so start early. The chapter on this subject provides a gentle way to view and approach this subject.

I should also point out that this book is not aimed at extolling the virtues of Buddhism nor written to convert anyone to Buddhism. It is but a simple illustration of Buddhist concepts to help us understand them and hopefully contribute in some small way towards our readers gaining the serenity and clarity to embrace life with all its guts and glory.

The last chapter should ideally be read with an adult as it is through discussion that these Buddhist concepts, as brought to life in the preceding chapters, become clear. Like most things, contemplation and discussion helps one gain a deeper understanding each time. Incidentally,

Tripitaka (used here as the surname of Lily, our chief protagonist) is the traditional term for Buddhist scriptures. Buddha's teachings were transmitted orally until about 500 BCE when some monks decided to write them down in case everyone died of famine and war (yes, really). So it is rather befitting I think, that here, much in the same spirit adopted all those centuries ago, this tinny, tiny illustrative snippet of some of Buddhism's basic concepts bears the same word Tripitaka.

ML Dempster

Oww That Hurt

The laws of causality (Karma)

Everything has a reason. And the
reasons have their reasons.

OWW THAT HURT

I t was a hot and sticky afternoon as Lily
shuffled along the pavement, kicking the
odd pebble along the way as she headed
towards the slightly shabby doors of Green
Cottage. She had just come home from school
and Mum had sent her straight out again to get
dinner from their local takeaway.

Lily sulked. Oh the injustice of it all! 'Why
couldn't Mum send Leah instead?' she thought
to herself, her sarcastic It's-Not-Fair-voice
playing in her head.

No, Mum had explained, Leah couldn't possibly go out to collect dinner (even though she
was the eldest in the family) because she had to
study for her eleven plus exams that were coming up.

'It's always Leah,' thought Lily bitterly,
'Leah, Leah, Leah! They don't care about me!'

Moodily she marched on, a petite firecracker of a nine-year-old with a straight razor-cut bob, vehemently kicking the odd coke can that dared lie in her way.

Presently the mouth-watering waft of roast duck mingled with the tempting smell of chips frying greeted Lily as she approached the small doors of Green Cottage.

An unassuming little place, it was tucked neatly between the grocer's and laundrette in a parade of shops next to West Finchley tube station.

Green Cottage was your usual Chinese takeaway - tinted doors and full length glass windows (also heavily tinted) giving little away of
its cosy interior with its worn formica counter,
dark panelled walls and row of foldable Ikea
chairs for waiting customers.

Orr-dorr *pease!*" snapped a prim old Chinese
lady behind the counter, beckoning Lily
impatiently.

"Hullo Aunty. I'm collecting," replied Lily

stepping forward unfazed. "Name's Tripitaka - half roast duck and vege".

"Ah.. *ok!*" the lady answered peering over her spectacles at a thick dog-eared exercise book that held details of all the orders.

"Still cooking, but nearly *dun!* You wait here, *pease!*" she continued, briskly waving Lily off towards the row of chairs without looking up. "*NEXT!*" she barked to the next customer, making him start.

Lily moved to the other end of the counter. She didn't sit on the chairs but stood, elbow resting on the counter, drumming her fingers impatiently.

"*Ai-yaaaa!*" came a voice from behind the counter, "What's that irritating noise ah?"

Lily jumped, startled, as she hadn't seen anyone there. On closer inspection, she could just make out the smooth, nut-brown top of a bald head emerging like a mini spaceship above the counter top.

The bald head gradually gave way to the sharp, twinkly eyes of an old man, followed by a humorous smile consisting of a very crooked, very yellowed and rather monstrous looking bank of protruding teeth - a combination which generally scared most little kids. Uncle had been sitting on a low wooden stool reading his Chinese newspaper behind the counter. He stood up stiffly, beaming at Lily.

"Uncle!" she admonished, dramatically patting her chest for effect, "You gave me a shock!"

Uncle was takeaway lady's husband and like his wife, was in his mid-seventies. As Lily had learnt from them, in Southeast Asia, everyone older than you were called Uncle or Aunty. It was as Uncle said, a way to remind the younger generation of their place in society and to *mind their manners*.

"Why so angry today, Ni Ni?" asked Uncle.

Ever since the day Lily stepped foot in the takeaway, Uncle had always called her Ni Ni, partly because she herself at the tender age of three (and not able to pronounce 'L's), had introduced herself as such and partly she suspected, because he didn't particularly like pronouncing 'L's either.

"My friend Evie hit me with her eraser," she replied, crumpling and uncrumpling her receipt furiously as she recalled what happened at school earlier, "...and I didn't start it."

Lily was visibly upset - and to think that day had started off rather well. Miss had let them watch the movie Labyrinth as part of their creative writing exercise much to Lily's glee as that meant less writing to do. However it was after lunch and PE that things really started to go downhill.

The girls had a little bit of a tiff in the playground during playtime and so by the time they came back to the classroom, they were all somewhat grumpy with each other. It was then, during the final

lesson of the day, that mean ol' Evie had flung her eraser at Lily. It had hit her squarely in the eye and smarted terribly.

"Ai-*yo*," continued Uncle, "So the eraser hit you. So why are you angry at Evie? Why aren't you angry at the eraser?"

Lily shot Uncle a bewildered stare.

"Because Evie threw the eraser,' she said hotly. "That's why I'm angry at her." She added a little indignantly, "The eraser didn't throw itself at me you know."

"Why do you think Evie threw the eraser at you?" asked Uncle, unperturbed.

Lily paused for a moment to think and then replied, "She was probably upset because Miss punished her for not paying attention during lesson."

It was true - Miss (short for Miss Duffy, their class teacher) had made Evie change her card a few minutes earlier as she was caught talking during lesson. If you changed your card twice in a week, you'd lose valuable playtime and you would be forced to sit indoors whilst others played outside. And if you were *really* naughty and got given a red card instead, you'd not only have to sit indoors but do so with your head resting in your arm, on the table facing downwards so you couldn't look at anything or talk to anyone. For anyone under the age of twelve, this kind of solitary confinement was the ultimate form of torture, so it was no wonder that most children kept out of trouble to avoid it.

"So Evie threw the rubber because she was angry her teacher punished her. So why aren't you angry at your teacher then?" probed Uncle innocently, giving his newspaper a quick shake to straighten it.

"Miss punished her because she was talking to Mia."

"O, I see," replied Uncle continuing to eye the contents of his paper. "So *Mia* is responsible then, not your teacher. Why are you not angry at Mia then?"

"But Evie was comforting Mia - Mia was upset because Ella pushed her during dodgeball at PE."

"Ah..HAH!" exclaimed Uncle triumphantly, "So it's *Ella's* fault then!" he continued with a twinkle in his eye.

But before Lily could answer back, the bell at the door gave a tinkle and in stepped Ella with her five year old little brother Alfie in tow. Ella had changed out of her school uniform already and being a bit of a tomboy, was dressed casually in her brother's hand-me-down Levi's and her favourite faded Arsenal FC jumper.

"Portion of chips please," Ella said, slapping two quid on the counter.

Aunty, who seemed to magically appear out of nowhere, slid the money deftly off it and disappeared into the back of the shop yelling what seemed to be Ella's order in Chinese.

"Oh hello," greeted Ella noticing Lily. "What are you doing here?"

Lily shrugged, "Dinner. My house isn't like yours Ella...no one wants to cook."

"Oh.. *you're* Ella," interrupted Uncle breaking into his toothy smile again. Those large incisors were frighteningly monstrous to the uninitiated. Little Alfie whimpered slightly at the sight - he'd never accompanied Ella to the takeaway before and this was his first encounter with Teeth and Uncle.

"Lily tells me you pushed your friend Mia. Why *har*?"asked Uncle, diving straight in as usual. Uncle never saw any point in conversational niceties.

"At PE?" asked Ella looking at Lily, seeking clarification.

"Yeah..," came the reply.

"Oh," said Ella, "didn't you know? The ball was heading towards the back of your head silly. I was trying to fend it off and I crashed into Mia instead by accident!"

"O.. like that *ah*?" piped up Uncle, his toothy grin beaming ever wider as he looked innocently from one girl to the other. Little Alfie edged ever so slightly behind his big sister.

There was a rather long pause as Lily began to assemble what actually happened there. So Ella didn't mean to hurt Mia - it was an accident really. And it had happened all because

Ella was trying to prevent the ball from hitting her in the first place! What an unexpected chain of events!

"I guess I can't really be mad at Evie," Lily said at long last.

"Loast duck and *kailan*!" announced Aunty loudly as she emerged from the back of the shop with a stack of steaming food boxes.

"Aiyah old man, what nonsense are you filling these children's heads with now?" she asked sternly, hands on her hips, looking at Uncle with tinge of good humour in her old eyes.

"Nothing old woman, none of your business," retorted Uncle, "Lily was just telling me she's angry at someone for doing something mean to her."

"Waste time getting angry at people," hurrumphed Aunty, looking at Lily. "Don't get angry - only waste energy! Like last week, *nah* - this boy threw big rock into shop window, broke glass, cost me £200 to fix! Tsk tsk tsk!" She clicked her tongue and shook her head dis-approvingly at the thought and expense.

"Weren't you angry at the boy, Uncle?" asked Ella.

"For a split second," started Uncle. "No," he corrected himself, remembering, "For *ten whole minutes* - yes, I was angry of course!"

Then he continued, "But then, you have to understand - the boy threw the stone because he was angry, in pain. He has his own problems. So I don't get upset over these sorts of things," he said, flashing a toothy grin at poor Alfie, "...otherwise get heart attack - *worse*!"

"Like your case," said Uncle peering closely at Lily, "you must understand there are reasons and events that caused what happened to you.

In life, one must understand the laws of cause and effect - every action has a reaction. Like NEWTON! You learn *Newton* at school? *Same thing*!"

Lily nodded, slightly doubtfully.

"Every action has a reaction and that reaction causes more reactions," explained Uncle. "This is called *karma*. When Ella accidentally hit Mia, Mia got upset. When Mia got upset, Evie tried to comfort her. When Evie tried to comfort her, Miss punished her for talking in class. When Miss punished Evie, Evie got upset and threw the eraser at you. Cause and effect - *karma*. You see?"

Lily pondered at what Uncle said. He went on, "But because you didn't realise that there were other things that caused Evie's actions, you got upset. But now that you understand that it was something *else* that caused her to act that way, you don't need to get angry, ya?"

"Yes, but what should I *do* about it?" asked Lily. She was beginning to understand how events had caused other events to occur and those in turn had ultimately caused Evie to throw the eraser at her. It made her feel better to know that Evie didn't throw the eraser at her out of spite, but that it was because she was upset at being ticked off by Miss and that too was caused by another event (Mia being pushed at PE) and so on. She didn't feel angry or upset anymore but she wasn't quite sure what to make of it all, now that she knew things happened as a result of other events before that.

"Well," continued Uncle, "once you understand karma, then you must tackle the *root of the problem*. And after you've done that, Buddha says you must *root out* all imprints of these bad feelings, these bad emotions from yourself … *remove* it! *Let it go*! ..like the song. You know the song *Let It Go*?"

Lily chuckled inwardly. Uncle was getting really passionate about this, she thought to herself. She had visions of him breaking out into song at the mention of 'Let it Go' and preferring not to tempt fate, didn't reply but instead quickly nodded in agreement.

"So how did you tackle the problem of the guy breaking your window then?" asked Ella, slightly amusedly. "Did you just '*let it go*'?"

"*No-lah!*" exclaimed Uncle indignantly. "I live Buddha's teachings, not *stupid*! I called the police of course! As I said, one must tackle root of the problem, so in this particular case, to tackle the problem, I reported it to the police. The police tracked him down from cctv and arrested him. So at least even if he doesn't learn his lesson, he'll think twice about doing it again. Imagine if he was allowed to continue breaking all the windows of all these shops here."

"Hmmm," nodded both girls in agreement as they collected their food. It seemed Uncle was not only wise but rather practical as well.

"Don't forget," called out Uncle as they headed for the door, "Buddha says one must get rid of all angry thoughts and emotions. So Lily, you must get rid of yours too."

"How?" asked Lily, recalling how her eye hurt when the eraser hit it and at that thought, began to feel resentment towards Evie all over again.

"FORGET ABOUT IT!" bellowed Uncle good humouredly. With that, he gave an even wider, more comical grin, proudly showing his enormous, wonky front incisors and bade the girls and a fleeing Alfie goodbye.

"Karma, karma, karma, karma, karma chameleon..." - the famous 1980s song from Boy George - is this what karma is, I hear you say? No, not really. But if you want to know a bit more about Karma, go to the final chapter - The-Preferably-To-Be-Read-With-An-Adult-Bit - and have a look at the section called The Second Noble Truth.

Joe Bordeaux

Wisdom and Compassion

It is by combining our intelligence and
emotion that we can transform our world
- Dalai Lama

JOE BORDEAUX

"**O**h bloomin' heck!!" exclaimed Lily, pinching her nose, "The *smell!*"

The 'smell' was emanating from a crumpled heap at a doorway to an upstairs flat, just next to Dicle Food Centre, the local grocer's.

The crumpled heap stirred and a brown, grubby arm stretched out to reveal the homeless man's face underneath.

"*C'mon*, let's *go*," insisted Ijeoma pulling Lily away. "He creeps me out."

"Oi," came a muffled reply, "who's creeping you out?"

A rather grimy face looked up and introduced himself, "...name's Joe."

Then the crumpled heap unfolded into a skinny, rather lanky man with dishevelled hair and a strong whiff of stale alcohol and pee about him.

He blinked at them blearily, his shamrock green eyes watery and slightly bloodshot. Joe looked a little over thirty although the amount of grime etched on the creases of the laughter lines of his face made him look much older.

"Er, hi," said Lily, slightly guiltily but still holding her breath.

"Come *on*," urged Ijeoma tugging even harder.

The three of them - Lily, Evie and Ijeoma - were on their way back from school and heading towards the local bus stop to catch their bus. To do this, they usually cut across the parade of shops that led towards the tube station as it was a shorter route. And today, that route happened to include one rather smelly tramp.

"Hang on a minute," drawled Joe, stretching a little more, "I don't s'pose any of you girls have spare change do yer?"

"No," came the curt reply from Ijeoma, "we were just going." With a determined flick of her carefully coiffured braids, she pushed Lily along. Ijeoma - loud, colourful and opinion-ated, didn't like anything that wasn't shiny or new or branded and this dirty, smelly tramp could not be more opposite to the qualities she held dear to her heart.

"Surely you could spare a quid for a hungry man?"

"Er..," ventured Lily hesitating, making Ijeoma's task of urging her on like trying to push a broken down car uphill.

"We're not supposed to talk to strangers," hissed Ijeoma fiercely to Lily and with a final push, managed to get her and the others to-wards the bus stop.

It was a typical grey November afternoon - cold, windy, with the hint of rain looming in the air. Autumn with its vibrant falling swathes of gold and russet leaves had come and gone, leaving the trees bare and unfriendly. Evie shivered slightly - the bus stop provided little shelter from the brisk wind blowing their way.

"Gosh it's cold," complained Evie, rubbing her arms in attempt to generate some heat. "He must be cold too," she continued recalling Joe.

"And hungry," added Lily.

"We should probably do something about it," said Evie thoughtfully.

"But he's a stranger!" protested Ijeoma. "And he could be a weirdo…"

"Yes, but we're Minnie Vinnies of our school," answered Lily, "and Minnie Vinnies are supposed to help people. Did you notice how hungry he looked? And his hands were shaking, did you see? And winter's coming so it's going to get even colder soon."

"Lily's right," said Evie, making up her mind. "We're supposed to help people and I'm going to see if I can help him."

That night, Evie tossed and turned in bed, unable to fall asleep. She racked her head, thinking about the Joe and his predicament. What could she do to help? He was obviously hungry and cold, and didn't have the means to buy his own food.

After much deliberation and weighing up of various options, she got out of bed, tiptoed to the dresser and quietly took out her piggy bank tucked in the back underneath the socks. It contained the money she had been saving for the last six months for a brand new bike.

It had not been easy to accumulate that amount. This precious hoard was the culmination of a lot of self-discipline - a multitude of unsuccumbed offers for lollies, sweets, birthday money and the untouched fifty euros from Grandma Rosie in Dublin which could have meant a few awesome visits to Flipperdoodle, the trampoline park.

"Well, it's for a worthy cause I guess," she thought to herself as she emptied out the cash and stuffed it into her school trouser pocket. "This should feed him for at least a few months 'til after winter I reckon," she thought, basing her calculations on two MacDonald's meals a day, before jumping back into bed and finally falling into slumber.

The next day, the girls were again walking back from school. They passed the same route they took the day before and when they walked by Joe again, he gave them a friendly wave. The girls gave a quick nod to acknowledge and walked past. But just as they were about to cross the road, Evie turned back abruptly, hurriedly fished out a wad of cash from her pocket and shoved them into Joe's hands.

Before the surprised man could utter a word, she walked off and joined her friends who were by now, looking on curiously.

The following week, the girls were once again walking home from school together. As they approached the Dicle Food Centre, they were once more met with a friendly 'hi' from Joe.

"I don't s'pose you've got any spare change have yer?" came the same question from bleary-eyed Joe.

"WHATT?" remarked Evie sharply, "What about the two hundred quid I gave you last week?"

"You gave him *two hundred quid*?" exclaimed Lily and Ijeoma together incredulously.

"Yes, I did," Evie answered, "I figured he could get food each day 'til the worst of winter was over."

"Yesssth," Joe chimed in, slightly slurring in his words, "she was kind enough to give me some money."

"Well, what did you do with it?" asked Evie hotly.

"I had the most amazzzing dinnerr at Ambiente," drawled Joe. "And the most fantabulllous bottle of wine in a long time," he continued, suddenly producing an almost empty bottle of french Bordeaux from under his blanket with a flourish.

"You spent ALL of that money in one meal??" wailed Evie. "That was supposed to last you a few months! I saved and scrimped for that money and you blew it all on ONE MEAL??"

"But I'd never had a posh meal before, and it's always been my *dream* to eat in *Ambiente*," protested Joe. "They even opened the place up for me on Sunday when I showed them all my money." Evie slapped her forehead in despair.

"I bet!" scoffed Lily. "They would've pushed the red carpet out for you for twenty quid, never mind two hundred."

"Oh *flippin' 'eck!*" wailed Evie, adding faintly, "My bike money..!"

"Well, it's too late now," stammered Joe,

beginning to sense that he had perhaps not done the right thing, "But I still have this bottle of wine… lushhhh!" He dribbled slightly before taking a swig of it and collapsing back on the floor.

"I'm sorry," he continued, "I think I may have let you down. But could you spare me a quid please? It's awfully cold these days and I could save up for a hot MacDonald's meal or something. Evie's face screwed up in pain as the girls walked on hurriedly.

A few days passed and the cold grey blustery days soon gave way to snowy showers. The girls spotted Joe huddling desperately in the doorway, trying to keep warm. None said a word but they were all thinking the same thing and wondering how on earth Joe would survive the freezing cold.

The following day, as they walked past Joe again, Ijeoma surprised them all by producing a pair of shoes and a man's padded jacket from her bag. She thrust them into Joe's arms and ran onwards to rejoin her friends on route towards their bus stop.

"Thank you!" hollered Joe after them, waving gratefully.

Their happiness however, was short-lived as the very next day, when they walked past Joe again, they noticed he was clad in his usual clothes, tattered wool blanket with not a jacket in sight. To top it all off, he had one shoe missing.

"Where's your jacket Joe?" snapped Ijeoma accusatively, "and where's the other shoe from the pair I gave you?"

"Uh," sniffled Joe, stretching out stiffly. "I uh,.. about that..," he continued scratching his head a little sheepishly.

"*Well*?" continued Ijeoma, tapping her foot impatiently.

"Well, y'see," mumbled Joe, "I wasssth over at Ambiente again lasssth night, hoping they'd top up me bottle," he continued, holding up the now empty bottle of Bordeaux, "Mmmmm,.. lllluushhhhh…"

Joe lifted up the bottle, jiggling it over his mouth, trying to extract any remaining drops of wine.

"But they were veeerrrrry unfriendly this time," he continued, "veeeeerrrry shhhtrange. Before I knew it, some big guy picked me up and pushed me offff," cried Joe indignantly.

"Lasthh thing I know was I woke up back here but I can't remember where I put my jacket or where the other shoe isssth. Hmmm, ssshhh-trange…" He scratched his head dubiously.

"Oh JUMPIN' JOLLOF!!!" exclaimed Ijeoma, annoyed beyond belief, "you *lost* the jacket *and* shoes? That was my dad's Burberry jacket - *Burberry*! And those shoes were Timberland - *Timberland!* And what use is one shoe anyway??" Ijeoma flung her hands in the air frustratedly - didn't these people know how to appreciate quality brands? Ughhh!

"Well, why did you give them to him then?" ventured Evie, "if you knew they were expensive?"

"Well, I thought he'd take better care of them," said Ijeoma bitterly. "Why did *you* give him the two hundred pounds then? It's not like he made good use of *that* either!" Evie shot her a withering look.

"Well, I didn't know he was gonna splurge the whole amount on one bloomin' meal, was I??" she argued, her voice getting louder and more irate by the minute.

"Well, I didn't know he was going to flippin' *lose* the clothes on his back, was I?" retorted Ijeoma, well and truly wound up by now.

"Well, it's *your* fault for getting us to do something to 'help' him in the first place," exclaimed Evie looking at Lily accusatively. "We would never have got into this mess if you didn't go on about our bloomin' Minnie Vinnies code and all that!"

"HEY!" snapped Lily, "I didn't make you give him all your savings!" The trio walked briskly, their heated exchanges getting louder and louder and more and more argumentative. By the time they reached Green Cottage, their bickering had reached fever pitch.

"AIYAAAHHHH...!" came a familiar voice from behind the counter, "What's all this noise ah? Why so angry?"

It was Uncle, takeaway Aunty's husband, sitting behind the counter, picking beansprouts and watching a rather small, discrete-looking telly in front of him. He was sitting on a low child's stool, deftly nicking off the fibrous root ends of each bean sprout before dropping the now pristine white sprout into a bowl of water on his side.

The girls all started to tell him what had happened, all at once: "...that was my bike money! How could he have spent it all in one go?"

"...he had lost the coat the very next day! It was a *Burberry*! How can anyone lose a Burberry??"

"..even if he ate three times a day at Mac-Donald's, it would've lasted him 'til January!"

"... my dad's now asking where his shoes have gone..!"

"AIYAH!!! ENUFFFF!!!" exclaimed Uncle, shaking his head vigorously having miraculously got the gist of what had happened from three raving girls all talking at the same time. The girls stopped and looked at him expectantly.

Composedly Uncle continued, "It's simple," he said, waving them to calm down.

"It's good you all wanted to help - you are kind." He continued, "*Good* kids! You have compassion, meaning you care for others. *Very* good! But compassion is not enough, you must also have *wisdom*. That's what you forgot here!"

The girls looked at him questioningly.

"In life," explained Uncle, "compassion

should always be accompanied by wisdom. The two must go hand in hand,... like this game show!"

He grinned, flashing his massive toothy smile for a second, then pointed vigorously at the the telly, "Like BRITAIN'S MOST DESERVING! You watch *Britain's Most Deserving*? *Same thing*!"

The girls shook their heads, puzzled. Uncle said the oddest things sometimes. He then proceeded to explain to them the rules of the game.

"So - there are three contestants. Each will tell the audience a bit about their situation and the audience decide who to award the prize money to. Like today's contestants - Jim, Bob and Julie...*see*?"

The show flicked to a recording of each contestant with the host - Desi Denny's voice-over in the background telling the audience about them.

First up was Jim, shown driving his lorry. Jim worked for a large distributer, driving lorries across the Channel to France and back. He lived with his invalid mother caring for her. Jim doesn't earn much, just enough for himself and his mum.

Next was Bob who was unemployed. Bob lost his job two years ago and his wife had taken his kids away with her. The film switched to Bob sitting in his cardboard box outside WHSmith, chatting to Des and telling him how desperate he was to see his kids and be a good father.

Lastly, Julie the trainee accountant. She came here from Vietnam ten years ago on a boat with other refugees. She lives with her sister in a house share in London.

"So in this gameshow, the audience decide

who of the three contestants deserves to win the £60,000 prize money!" explained Uncle.

"*Ooooooh*," exclaimed Ijeoma, "That's a lot of money!"

"Yes," continued Uncle, "but HAH! There's a catch! The audience are not told what the contestants will do with the prize money until *after* they have decided the winner! Only then do they reveal to the audience what they intend to use the money for."

The game show went on, showing footage of the contestants' daily lives, where they lived and where they worked (apart from Bob of course, whom they showed sitting outside his patch on the high street).

"So," asked Uncle, with an impish twinkle in his eye, "who do you think should get the money?"

"Bob," said Ijeoma without hesitation, "'cos he's the worst off of them all."

"Yeah," seconded Lily and Evie, "Bob - he needs the money the most."

"Jim and Julie don't have much either but they can take care of themselves 'cos both have jobs already," added Lily.

"Yeah, I'd give it to Bob. Look he's sleeping in a cardboard box and he's crying because he misses his kids so much," agreed Evie.

"You think so ah?" asked Uncle, "let's see then. *Look*! They are going to vote now."

The girls crowded over the counter eagerly as the host Desi, announced the winner: "..and the winner is,... BOB!!"

The audience erupted into cheers and claps.

"HAH!" exclaimed Uncle triumphantly, " I told you they'll get it wrong!"

"But why...?" started Evie before being shushed by Uncle. She didn't understand why Uncle thought the wrong person won.

"Look! *Nah*! They're each going to reveal to the audience what they're intending to use the prize money for. This is the interesting bit!"

Desi then announced to the audience, "Now folks, here are the earlier interviews with our lovely contestants revealing what they're going to do with the prize money if they were chosen by you..."

The show switched to earlier recordings of each of the contestants. First up was Jim.

"Uh, well," Jim started gruffly, trying to suppress his emotions, "If I win the sixty grand, I'd take Mum on a holiday, somewhere nice like Venice..."

Jim cleared his throat a little, then continued, "The remainder will go towards getting someone to care for her when I'm away on me jobs - just to make sure she's all right. Like the last time I was away, she had a fall and couldn't call for help. Luckily I was due back that day, wasn't I Mum?" he continued, looking at someone behind the camera. The camera panned out to include Jim's mum; a sweet, diminutive, frail looking woman in a wheelchair, smiling. Some of the audience could be heard murmuring a slightly regretful "Awww…"

Next came Bob's recording. He was sitting at the homeless shelter canteen, talking to Desi.

"I love my kids so much y'know, and I miss them so much. The missus is always sayin' I can't have them with me cos I can't take care of them."

Bob sniffles a little, "This time if I win the money, I'm taking all of us on a five star holiday to Malaga! I'm gonna SPEND IT ALL! BLOW IT ALL ON ME AN' THE KIDS! Lucy and Jojo will get to buy *all* the clothes and toys they want - no expense spared! That'll teach *her* to say I'm completely irresponsible and can't take care of em!" exclaimed Bob, miffed. He added, nodding smugly, "I might even buy myself some of them smart Polo shirts too. I think I *deserve* it don't you?"

The camera then panned out and switched to Julie's recording.

Julie, dressed in a simple jumper and jeans, spoke to the camera shyly, almost hesitantly.

"I came to the UK when I was ten - me, my parents and my older sister. We had travelled by boat for months before finally reaching London," she said. "We lived in various places: hostels, shelters, sometimes in a single room for months on end when the council couldn't find any available housing. I managed to get a scholarship to study accountancy and graduated last year. I'm working now and can help support my family. If I win the prize, I will be using it to help keep the local community centre going. I have been helping them run the place for the last few years as well as doing their accounts for free. I know the extra money will in fact get them up and running permanently as opposed to being opened only whenever funds are available. We estimate we'll be able to help about a hundred people each month with hot meals, free haircuts and access to help and advice."

Julie's recording ended. The audience was silent. There was a palpable sense of remorse in the atmosphere, the type coming from the *wrong choice being made.*

"JUMPIN' JOLLOF! They should have chosen Julie!" exclaimed Ijeoma, her voice tinged with regret.

"Bob's just going to waste it and he'll be back where he started in no time," moaned Evie, hands in the air. "*Eejits*! If they had given it to Julie, she would've helped more people and perhaps even people like Bob!"

"Yes," chuckled Uncle, "I told you they'd get it wrong - most people do. People have compassion which is a good thing but many forget compassion goes hand in hand with wisdom. Sometimes to be kind, one has to look beyond the obvious - the most attractive solution may not be the correct one."

"Like your case," continued Uncle, returning to picking his beansprouts, "you are good girls, all of you, wanting to help this chap outside there."

"So how can we help him? We've tried everything but failed," gloomed Evie, still in mourning over her evaporated bike dreams.

"I've got a bit of pocket money," volunteered Lily hesitantly, "but I'm not sure I want to give that to Joe now that I know he might not use it wisely. Uncle, what *should* we do?"

"Well," answered Uncle, "why don't you do this instead?" And with a stiff "Aiyah" and a grunt, he stood up, leafed through some papers until he found what he was looking for and handed it to Lily.

"Here," he said, giving her a leaflet and then passing her a box of piping hot sweet sour chicken and rice. "Why don't you donate that pocket money of yours to this charity," he said pointing at the leaflet. "It's called St Martin's and it's a charity for the homeless. Also tell your Joe fella he can have this sweet sour chicken if he looks at the leaflet."

The girls left the takeaway and walked down the parade of shops to where Joe was sitting, and did as Uncle suggested.

A week later, when the three were walking back from school, they noticed Joe and his blanket and box were no longer there. In fact they never saw him again after that.

Then a month later, having seen no sign of Joe anywhere, the girls all wondered what had happened to him. Lily asked Uncle if he knew what had become of Joe. Uncle smiled and showed them a crumpled envelope - it contained a photo of Joe, all clean shaven, smiling and apparently working at the kitchen wearing a St Martin's t-shirt.

"The leaflet you gave him contained St Martin's telephone number and directions," explained Uncle smiling. "Looks like he found his way there after all."

Wisdom and compassion - like Ebony and Ivory (yet another classic song!) - live together in perfect harmony. Both go hand in hand. To find out more, have a look at the chapter The Preferably-to-be-Read-with-an-Adult Bit at the end of the book.

The Luckiest Girl

The Origin of Suffering

You yourself, as much as anybody in the
entire universe, deserve your love and affectiom
- Buddha

THE LUCKIEST GIRL

T he girls chattered excitedly amongst themselves as they spilled out of the school grounds that afternoon. Spirits were high - it was Friday and to cap it off, they were all going back to Lily's for a sleepover! Ah, what plans they had - not sleeping 'til 3am (obviously!), midnight feasts, pranking and the ever mandatory makeovers.

"L-O-L!" giggled Evie, "Lily, did you see what Lizzy packed in her bag?"

Lizzy opened the zip and surreptitiously flashed the insides of her knapsack at Lily. Further giggles and snorts of suppressed laughter erupted amongst the five girls.

"Tee hee," chortled Mia, "wonder who's going to get pranked with shaving foam this time!"

All five friends - Lily, Evie, Mia, Ijeoma and Lizzy - made their way towards Lily's house which was just a few bus stops from their school. It was half-term which meant no school for the coming week, which was also why Lily was allowed to host a sleepover.

A little while later, the girls reached Lily's home which she shared with her parents and older sister, Leah. It was a three-bed, red-bricked Victorian terrace and like most London suburbs, had a long back garden, flanked on all three sides by neighbouring gardens.

Lily rubbed her hands in glee, thinking of the antics to come. Tonight, there would be lots of creeping about, trying not to annoy Leah (who would invariably be holed up in her bedroom like most teenagers, listening to music) and if previous sleepovers were anything to go by, never mind there was a additional mattress laid out at the foot of her bed, by the wee hours of the morning, they would all be asleep, bunched up and lying like a row of cramped sardines on Lily's little bed.

After dinner, some trampolining in the garden and countless games, the girls settled down in Lily's bedroom. They had finished watching two movies already and at a quarter to midnight, had been reminded by Lily's parents for the umpteenth time to *go to sleep*.

The room was dark, lit only by the unpredictable flashes of light from the pocket torch as it was passed from one girl to the other.

"What shall we do next?" whispered Evie conspiratorially.

Mia gave a wide yawn, "Sleep?"

"No," nudged Lizzy, "not yet! Let's play a game."

"Ho hum.. we've played Dobble and Snap already. I'm all gamed out," said Ijeoma, snuggling into her sleeping bag. "Let's just talk."

"Okay," replied Lily pulling her blanket closer. "What shall we talk about?"

"Crushes," giggled Lizzy, the girliest of them all. "Let's talk about crushes. I think Rocco has a crush on you Mia..."

"Whaat?" protested Mia, reddening. "That's so not true!"

"Yes it is," retorted Evie and promptly did an impersonation of Rocco running his fingers through his hair. The girls burst into peals of laughter. It was true - Rocco did that every time he saw Mia.

"In fact," continued Evie, "Rocco's not the only one…"

"Oooh," teased Lizzy, "I bet it's Tom!"

"Stop it, you guys," replied Mia, blushing more than ever. Mia always turned bright red whenever she felt overly self-conscious.

"Well, it's true Mia," replied Lily, "all the boys like you 'cos you're pretty."

'Mia's so lucky,' Lily thought to herself with a pang of jealousy. 'The boys all do what she tells them to because she's the prettiest girl in the class. If only that were me'.

She thought about her own looks: Being of mixed heritage - part Chinese, part Filipino and part Spanish, she was the polar opposite of Mia when it came to the looks stakes. Whilst Mia was blonde, fair and sweet-faced, Lily by contrast had jet black hair, worn in a sharp bob that framed the two large, dark pools which made up her eyes. Her features although distinctly delicate - a little button nose set in a refined oval face - were contrasted by an expressive set of pouty lips and together with her rosy colouring gave one the impression of intense vibrancy and life. She was, though she didn't know it, strikingly beautiful in an unconventional way.

"I wish I was pretty," sighed Lizzy enviously. The oldest in the class, Lizzy was easily also the tallest. Tanned with unruly frizzy hair which she frequently wore long and loose, she was developing into a teenager slightly earlier than the rest and consequently was beginning to look a bit gangly. She looked at Mia who looked gorgeous even in her pyjamas and sighed, "You are so lucky Mia, you're the lucki-est girl in our class!"

"Yeah," agreed Lily, "I think you're the *lucki-est* one amongst all of us!"

Mia shook her head. "Really?" she answered, really surprised. She paused and chewed her plait agitatedly.

"But it's *awful*!" she suddenly blurted out. "It's so *pressurising* to stay pretty and I'm al-ways so self conscious about the way I look; what I wear, if my hair's ok... I'm always afraid that if I don't look nice, people won't like me anymore!" She heaved a big sigh and looked al-most relieved after her sudden confession.

"Oh, I've always wished I was popular like *you* Evie!" she continued, pouring out what seemed to be pent up inside her. "You're just yourself and everyone likes you for who you are. You don't have any pressure, you don't have to keep up appearances, you're free as a bird! I think *you're* the luckiest girl amongst all of us!"

The girls looked at Mia, surprised at the sud-den outburst and even more surprised at what she had just revealed. They had no idea until now, what it felt to be in Mia's shoes. All this time, they had thought she revelled in being the prettiest girl. It didn't occur to them 'til now, that what they saw as a gift all this time, was in fact a burden to Mia.

"You're so confident, Evie," Ijeoma piped up turning to Evie, "and funny."

"..and quirky," added Lily.

"..and you get along with everyone," said Lizzy. "That's why you're popular and everyone wants to be your friend."

"I have to say I was a little envious when you got school councillor," confessed Lily. "You didn't even have to prepare your speech as everyone was going to vote for you anyway. *You're* the luckiest one of all!"

The girls all nodded in agreement. Evie was indeed the most popular kid at school. She was petite, had chestnut hair which she frequently wore in plaits and a smattering of freckles that sat just below her bright Irish eyes. Evie always had an easy going way about her, which endeared her to not only her peers but to the adults as well - *all* the mums loved Evie.

"The thing is," ventured Evie shyly, "I've always envied *you*," she said, glancing at Ijeoma.

"*Me*??" exclaimed Ijeoma incredulously. "Why me?"

"Yes, you," nodded Evie. "You have your brothers and sisters to play with. I'm an only child and I'm always with my aunts at the salon if I'm not with my parents. I never ever have anyone my age to play with. Your house is always exciting, loud, crazy, noisy and full of fun. Mine's full of Old People, if you know what I mean..."

"Yeah, I know the feeling," nodded Lizzy. Lizzy too knew what it was like to be the only child - it was something only an only child would ever understand. The pros were great of course - one never had to share anything. You always had your parents' undivided attention and you never had to compete for the spotlight with a sibling. In short you were always the centre of your parents' universe. That was the cushy part. The bad part was of course, that you were constantly surrounded by adults and treated as one, which was different to having someone your age to play or argue with.

"Well," continued Evie, "truth be told, I've always wanted to be *you* Ijeoma. You're never lonely, you have your brothers and sisters, your life is always exciting and fun. I've always thought *you* were the luckiest girl in our class!"

"You're crazy," exclaimed Ijeoma, laughing. "I can't believe it! Since we're all coming out with our secrets anyway, I might as well own up - I've *always* been envious of you Lizzy!"

"What? Why?"

"Cos you're *rich*!" declared Ijeoma. "You never have to give up buying stuff you want because it's too expensive: '*we can't buy three of everything Joma*' or '*you don't need that Joma, you can use Jay's old one when he finishes with it.*' You have an amazing life Izzy - you get to buy whatever you like from Muggles, you're forever going on holiday trips to Italy and you can get anything and everything your heart desires. *You're* the luckiest girl in our class!"

Lizzy was taken aback. She had no idea this was how her friends saw her. It was true she could afford some of things her friends couldn't and it was true her parents never deprived her of anything she wanted - even extravagant requests like buying overpriced stationery from Muggles which Lily's mum *never* allowed Lily. It was something she had always taken for granted and never really thought about 'til now. But oh, what didn't they know was that she would have given all that up in a heartbeat if *only* that meant her parents got back together and didn't go through with the divorce. However deep down in her heart, Lizzy knew the fighting would start all over again so it was probably best for everyone if Dad and Mum lived separately.

"I don't think I'm that lucky," Lizzy said quietly, recalling the times Dad and Mum constantly fought each other. "I'm always shuttling between Dad and Mum. Those holidays you talk about - that's also how Dad and Mum 'share' me. So one half term I'm with Dad in Italy, the next with Mum somewhere else. Sometimes I feel like a piece of property tussled between two people. It's not as great as you all think it is."

She looked at Lily, grinned and said matter-of-factly, "I've always wished I lived *your* life - you're smart, pretty, you have a perfect family, both parents who are together, who love you. You have the perfect life, Lily. *You're* the lucki-est girl of all!"

The girls looked round at each other. A million thoughts running apace through their minds - they were each thinking about their circumstances and also that of each other's.

"GROUP HUG!" blurted out Lily and they all moved closer in unison and hugged each other hard.

 "We're *all* lucky after all!" exclaimed Ijeoma. "We just didn't know it!" The girls laughed happily, counted their blessings and hugged each other again, each happy and grateful for their lives. And each of them decided secretly that *she* was the luckiest girl in the world.

Examination Woes

The Acceptance of Suffering and Mindfulness

Pain is inevitable, suffering is optional
- Haruki Murakami

EXAMINATION WOES

I t was half past four by the time Lily reached home and she was absolutely starving. The bus had been late today due to roadworks at Whetstone which meant the half hour journey home from school took twice as long.

She burst into the house, slammed the door and kicked off her shoes furiously.

"OI! Stop slamming the door and making such a racket - PEOPLE ARE STUDYING HERE!" hollered a very annoyed Leah from upstairs.

Leah, Lily's elder sister, was a year older and due to sit her eleven plus exams next week. Tall, thin and reserved, she was the polar opposite to her firecracker of a sister.

The eleven plus examinations were entrance exams which children of that age took to gain admission into certain secondary schools. Competition was fierce and with the scarcity of good schools in built-up urban areas such as theirs, not doing well enough in the eleven plus meant, according to Mum, 'ending up in a crap secondary school with kids who were either truants or troublemakers'.

"I'M NOT SLAMMING THE BLOOMIN'
DOOR!" Lily yelled back, yanking the piano
stool out from under the piano with an al-
mighty, toe-curling screech. She then sat down
and proceeded to play a thunderous rendition
of Holst's *Jupiter*.

As the deafening notes reverberated around
the house, one could just about make out
the sound of Leah stomping down the stairs
furiously.

"What the *hell* do you think you are doing?" she seethed, "Can't you see I'm studying? My exams are next week!"

The pummelling on the keys stopped momentarily.

"Well, my piano exam's next week too," Lily retorted coolly, "so I have to practise."

She turned her back abruptly at Leah and continued with her vociferous assault on the ivory keys, this time on a very lively *Allegretto*.

"Oh FUDGE!" howled Leah, shaking her fists exasperatedly. "You are *impossible*! I'm telling Mum!!"

"FINE!" Lily answered back, shouting above the din, "*Go on* then..." Which made Leah even madder.

"MUUUUMMMM!!!" Leah yelled.

Mum appeared from the kitchen, soap suds on her hands. The girls could tell from her face that she was in no mood to entertain their bickering.

"What is the matter with you two?" she snapped.

"I can't write my essay in all this noise!"

"But I've got my piano exam next week and *Allegretto* keeps getting worse and worse," wailed Lily welling up, "My fingers are now stumbling! Mum, I'm going to *fail*!!!"

"Well I've got entrance exams next week," persisted Leah, "If I fail, then it's the *end* of the world - I'm *finished!*" Her voice cracked into a sob.

"Well neither of you are going to achieve any-thing with all this noise," finished Mum sternly. "Lily, go and do your homework first. You can continue with piano later."

"You *always* take her side," protested Lily angrily, bursting into tears, "She *always* gets priority! It's just not fair! I HATE YOU TWO!!!" Kicking the piano stool aside, she stormed out of the house.

Furiously wiping her tears along the way, Lily found herself walking towards the corner shop.

'I'll get a Kit Kat', she thought, trying to soothe herself, 'maybe a Calippo too.'

Presently the delicious smell of chips wafting from Green Cottage beckoned, pushing aside all thoughts of chocolate. She remem-bered how hungry she was and so walked into the ever familiar takeaway instead.

"Orr-dorr *pease!*" snapped Aunty behind

the counter without looking up, as she approached.

"Portion of chips please Aunty," requested Lily, sniffing and breathing slightly jaggedly as she handed over some money.

Uncharacteristically, Aunty looked up and flashed a piercing but slightly concerned look at Lily. Then equally quickly, she looked back down, put the money into the cashier and scurried off into the back barking instructions to the cook in Chinese.

"Hullo Ni Ni," came the familiar voice of Uncle, takeaway Aunty's husband.

Uncle was sitting on his low stool behind the counter watching telly, rhythmically pummelling his aching shoulders with his fist.

"Hello Uncle."

"How's it going?"

Lily shrugged and sniffed despondently.

"Hmmm," continued Uncle, standing up with a stiff grunt. He peered a little closer, his large teeth slightly protruding beneath the beginnings of a smile and asked, "What's the matter?"

Lily heaved a big sigh. It was a long, heavy sigh, the type one gave when faced with an insurmountable mountain or a deep chasm too deep to be crossed.

"*I can't do it*!" she burst out suddenly, tears welling up, "I've got a piano exam next week and the more I practise, the more my fingers seize up and stumble. I can't do it! I'm going to FAIL!!"

Trying to catch her breath in between sobs, she blubbered on, "And Leah's no better. She's so stressed with revision at the moment because her entrance exams are next week too. Her practice tests scores seem to worsen with each test she does. *And* we're just at each other's throats, fighting all the time at the moment. It's awful *!* Oh how I *wish* exams didn't exist!"

"Well," said Uncle thoughtfully, "in that case, you need to know archery."

"Huh?"

"Ar-cherrr-ree," repeated Uncle loudly as if Lily was hard of hearing. "You know archery? Bow and arrow? Your problem is like archery...*same thing*!"

As always Uncle said the most peculiar things.

"Here, I show you," he continued, lifting the counter flap to let her in to the back of the shop.

"This way," pointed Uncle as they walked through the kitchen and into the small garden courtyard at the back, past Aunty who was rattling off in some Chinese dialect to a jumpy cook and his assistant, both of whom were chopping vegetables and nodding their heads vigorously. Lily looked on interestedly as she walked past, taking in the tiny but spotless kitchen with its huge wok in the middle pulsating like a red-hot beating heart. Even from where she was, she could feel its intense heat fuelled by the powerful rocket-roaring flames beneath and above, soft, puffy, steaming clouds laden with the mouth-watering smell of sizzling garlic and ginger.

The courtyard was a small but lovely little sun trap. It was also full of pots and planters of every shape and colour, housing a sizeable collection of climbers, evergreens and scented plants. And flitting amongst the abundance of blooms and foliage were a multitude of butterflies and bees, busily darting here and there, from flower to flower, bustling just like the cooks back in the kitchen.

"Wow," breathed Lily. She had no idea such a beautiful little paradise existed at the back of Green Cottage.

"*Nah!*" pointed Uncle towards an ancient twisted wisteria by the back wall. Lily stared blankly in front of her.

"Huh?"

"Archery," said Uncle, pointing again.

"Oh!" exclaimed Lily, suddenly realising that Uncle was not indicating at the cascading purple blooms but rather at a target attached to the wall.

"Nice," Lily continued a little hesitantly, "but I don't see what this has got to do with exams..."

Uncle paused and held out his hand to a blue

swallowtail which settled lightly on his palm.

"See this fragile little butterfly…," he murmured softly, turning his palm slightly to have a closer look at the gleaming, blue beauty. "It's flying around amongst these flowers, just like you going through life. See those birds on the rooftops and flying overhead? All the time this butterfly's flying around, it is exposed, open to attack by all these hungry birds. Similarly, everyday at school, you are exposed to challenges and exams, and there's not a lot you can do about that."

"Do you think," he chuckled, "this butterfly worries all the time if it would be eaten up, just like you're worried all the time that you're going to fail?"

"Well, this wouldn't be the case if there weren't exams to start with. Oh if *only* they never existed."

Uncle grunted and examined the swallowtail further.

"Well I'm afraid that's not possible Ni Ni," he said. "That's the First Noble Truth - suffering exists. You must accept that. Not accepting this is the cause of your suffering. You suffer because you don't want to accept that these dreaded exams exist and you are fighting that idea. One must firstly accept exams, hardships, misfortunes, accidents - all this is part and parcel of life."

"Grade 1 was so much easier. Why oh why can't Grade 2 be just as easy?" continued Lily gloomily.

"You see," said Uncle as the swallowtail flew off, "again you are expecting life to be the same, easy all the time. Constant, no change. But nothing in life is constant. Life is sometimes easy, sometimes hard. It's like the sea - sometimes you have gentle currents, sometimes you get big waves. You see," he said with a pause and a chuckle, "You cannot expect things to go *swimmingly well* all the time."

"So," said Uncle, grabbing a bow and arrow neatly tucked away in a tall flowerpot serving as a quiver, "back to ar-cher-ree."

He handed them to Lily who held the bow hesitantly, unsure of what to do with it. What on *earth* was Uncle on about?

"You see," continued Uncle, ignoring her bewildered looks, "to alleviate suffering, one must practice Mindfulness. Do you know *Mindfulness*?"

Lily shook her head. Now Uncle had really lost it with all this eastern mumbo jumbo, she thought. Noble Truths and now Mindfulness?

"People have forgotten how to live in the present," continued Uncle, "animals haven't."

He pointed at the butterflies, "Those butter-flies haven't."

He paused to check the fins of the arrow before continuing, "You failing your exam next week is a just a thought - it is a projection of your fear. Is it real? *Have you failed*? No."

Lily pondered for a moment, absorbing what Uncle said. It was true - she hadn't failed her exam. She hadn't even had the exam yet. *She was simply afraid that she would fail.*

"Now lift the bow this way," said Uncle, guid-ing Lily. "Thumb around the string, middle finger over the thumb : this is called the Mongolian draw. Pull the arrow backwards, *strong*! Feel the tension of the string between your fingers."

Lily did as she was told. She felt the metal string taut between her fingers, the change in tension as she pulled it back further and the almost imperceptible metallic resonance as arrow slid across bow.

"Now look at the target and aim. Be aware of how you are holding the bow and arrow. Notice what you are doing. In your mind, see your arrow travelling through the air and hit-ting the middle of the target. Focus, *feel* - there is nothing else but your fingers, the bow and arrow. Nothing else in this world exists at this moment."

Lily listened. And as she took aim, it was as if the world around her - the buzzing garden, the chirping birds, the clanking of the wok, the chatter in the kitchen - had suddenly turned down in volume. Muffled. Distant. Detached. It was just her, the bow and the arrow.

"Breathe...," said Uncle, "Now let go..."

Lily let the arrow fly. It whizzed across the courtyard, clipped the very top of the broad beans and landed just two rings shy of dead centre. She loosened her shoulders and gave a frustrated sigh.

"Not bad," said Uncle. "Now, try to recall what you did wrong just now - the bow slanted slightly too high? Slight wobble before letting go? Now this time, remember that and correct it. Then concentrate, be present and let go."

Lily took the bow up again, slid the arrow into position and took aim. This time, she felt alert, aware of every single flex of her arm, the angle of her arm, her wrist, her fingers, leading all the way to the tip of the arrow. It was as if she was the arrow.

Then taking a deep breath, she visualised the arrow taking off, the flight of its path from her wrist, all the way across the courtyard to the bulls eye.

Once again, the world around her tuned out

and ceased to be. The arrow hitting or missing the target ceased to matter, it wasn't even in her thoughts. She was, at that very moment, the arrow itself, ready to take the journey she visualised in her mind.

Then, with a smooth flick, she let go. The arrow sailed across, zipped past the broad beans, clearing their tops this time and landed firmly in dead centre - a perfect shot!

"WAHOOOO!" shrieked Lily, jumping up and down excitedly, "I DID IT!!!"

"Very good Ni Ni!"clapped Uncle, beaming widely, his large, wonky teeth protruding comically. "Now do you understand what you have to do for your exam?"he asked.

Lily nodded.

"I think so, Uncle," she said, thinking carefully. "Accept I have to do exams like everyone else. There's no point in trying to avoid or deny it."

Uncle nodded approvingly, "And what about failing your exam?"he asked.

"Don't get attached to fear," replied Lily, "I've not failed. It's fear - an emotion. It's not reality."

"Yes," agreed Uncle. "These are are just thoughts. Nothing more. They are not real so don't give them so much time and energy thinking about them until they become real to you. Now what about how to tackle your stumbling fingers?"

"Hmm," replied Lily thinking hard, "I think piano is like archery after all. I need to see in my mind's eye what I want to achieve, pay attention when I'm playing the music, practise and correct my mistakes. Then in the exam itself, focus and *just do it*."

"And *let go*," finished Uncle, patting her on the head. "At that point there is nothing more you can do."

Lily nodded.

"*Good*!" Uncle said, "You've got it! Remember, *do your best and forget the rest*! Don't think about whether you are going to pass or fail - you can't control that."

Uncle stood up with a stiff grunt and then murmured softly to himself, "We learn to be in the world as it is, to embrace tension, and to handle our thoughts and feelings. This is the Middle Way."

And as they both walked back to the front of the shop, Aunty gruffly handed Lily her chips with the barest hint of a smile lurking at the corner of her mouth. As stern and curt as she always seemed to be, Aunty actually had a heart of gold and never liked seeing children cry (unless they deserved it of course).

"Better now Lee Lee?" she asked, almost kindly. Lily nodded meekly.

"Good," replied Aunty. "Sometimes Uncle give good advice after all. But don't forget..."

"Forget what Aunty?"

"Don't forget... always *more* exams to look forward to tomorrow!" she cackled wickedly as Lily turned to leave the shop.

For more information on the practice of Mindfulness, go to the chapter The Preferably-to-be-Read-with-an-Adult Bit at the end of the book and look for the Fourth Noble Truth.

The Race of Life

Noble Eight-Fold Path : Right View

Don't compare yourself to others. Run
your own race as your finish line is not
the same place as anyone else's.

THE RACE OF LIFE

Next to the school were wide-open playing fields that led on to the green, manicured lawns of the Finchley Memorial Hospital. It was in these playing fields that the annual school Sports Day was held.

Lily and her friends were there practising for track and field with their PE teacher Mr Harold. It was a warm, sunny day and not a cloud was in sight to taint the gleaming blue sky. The fields were abuzz with the hum of insect life.

Lily sniffed the air. It was warm and grassy

with a hint of earthiness and she winced at the occasional whiff of wee-like odour coming from the elderflowers growing wild nearby. A gentle breeze kept the children pleasantly cool as they did their warm ups. There were a few dog walkers out that morning, perambulating along the footpaths that encircled the fields and in the distance a white husky lifted its hind leg to pee at one of the lamp posts alongside the footpaths. Some young mums were sitting out on the benches dotted round the edge with their prams and pushchairs, having a chat and enjoying the warm sunshine.

"RRRRIGHT! Gather round the start line please!" shouted Mr Harold, leaning rather perilously on one of his crutches trying to pick up his dropped hanky.

Mr Harold had unfortunately broken his leg playing football a month earlier, so training this lot for the hundred-metre race was proving a little tricky.

"Lily, Mia, Ijeoma, Tom and Harry, please arrange yourselves in a straight line," he continued trying to sound strict but ultimately failing to do so.

Strict Mr Harold was most certainly not. In fact, he was one of the children's favourite teachers. Medium-built, youngish, with dark hair and eyes and frequently attired in suits a size too large, he was today dressed more appropriately for his age in a tracksuit and t-shirt. The children adored Mr Harold as he never ever talked down to kids the way most adults and teachers did. To Mr Harold, they were equals and were treated as such.

"*Oh mah gawd,*" moaned Mia in a faked American accent, "I can't possibly beat Tom in this - he's way too fast!"

The other girls nodded, some giggling at the accent. Tom was indeed the fastest in their class. Small, wiry and brown as a berry, Tom was as nimble on the track as he was at maths and pretty much every subject taught.

"Well, you're pretty fast yourself," grinned Harry at Mia. "I'd say you have a chance."

Harry was the class heartthrob due to his good looks and boyish charm. All the girls found him irresistibly charming, no more so than Lily who often found herself speechless in his presence for some inexplicable reason.

"I don't know," said Mia to Harry, "Tom's fast and you've got stamina.."

"I think I'm gonna come last on Sports Day," sighed Lily surveying her mates. "I'm definitely not fast compared with you guys!"

"Don't worry Lily," said Ijeoma kindly. "I'm not great at running either. At least you're in the school play again this year. Bet Miss Quinn will select you to sing the solo again. You've got an amazing voice," she added a little enviously.

"Yeah," Tom chimed in, "you're really good at music. My violin on the other hand..." Tom made the gesture of wringing one's throat and the girls giggled at his silly portrayal of his violin skills.

"I wonder who's going to top the SATs next year," said Ijeoma, "it's going to be so nerve-wrecking!"

"Bet Tom and Lily will ace them," said Mia, "you guys are the brainiest."

"It's going to be awful for the rest of us," she added with a sigh, "we're going to fail."

"Now, what's all this talk about who's going to win and who's going to fail hmm?"said Mr Harold, hobbling closer to the huddle of children. "You shouldn't be comparing yourselves with each other. You should only compare with yourself so that you can better yourself."

"Yes, but Mr Harold, this is life *innit*?" chimed Harry, embellishing the last word with a hip hop hand gesture for effect. "There's always a winner and always a loser."

"*Loser*! *Loser*!" jibed Tom sticking a big 'L' up with his fingers and pulling a silly face.

The children laughed. However Mr Harold continued rather seriously, "As I said, there's no need to compare - there are no winners and there are no losers in life. Come on, I'll show you."

Beckoning them to come closer, Mr Harold positioned each of them along the starting line of the track, spaced an arm's length apart and proceeded to give each of them a few quiet words of instruction.

"RRRIGHT!" he said, "100 metres, *are ... you ... ready*?"

The children looked towards him and nodded, each with one knee slightly bent, arms in position and ready to sprint. Lily felt her heart thumping a million miles an hour in anticipation of the start whistle.

"*Ready.., steady..*, GO!" exclaimed Mr Harold.

And they were off! Straightaway Tom was out in front like a shot, sprinting his way past Harry who seemed to be taking his time, even smoothing his fringe and flashing Mia a taunting smile as he overtook her. Lily chuckled - Harry could be so vain, but oh so funny!

By now the air was terribly hot and dry. Dust motes danced wildly in the sunshine, stirred by the movement of the children and whipped further by the occasional breeze. Lily looked to her right - she and Ijeoma were neck and neck, pounding away and kicking up small clouds of dry grass seeds as they ran. It was all very exciting!

A hundred metres..., eighty metres.., fifty metres.., the seconds that passed as the children clocked up the distance seemed like an eternity.

Lily glanced to her right again. Panting furiously, Ijeoma was coming up the track with determination.

'Oh my goodness,' thought Lily to herself,

'look how quick she is! She's literally right next to me - I can even hear her breathing!' So preoccupied with Ijeoma that she forgot to focus on her own running, Lily stumbled. Seizing the opportunity, Ijeoma forged ahead past her.

"LAST TWENTY METRES!" yelled Mr Harold from afar, wobbling dangerously on his crutches, whistle perched near his mouth at the ready.

Tom turned anxiously to look behind him, worried that he would be overtaken at the last lap. He could see Harry charging up behind him and barely a few centimetres behind was Mia, face screwed up and red in determination not to be beaten by Harry. It was going to be a very close race indeed!

Even with his muscles burning like fire, Tom daren't slow down for even a bit for if he did, Harry would overtake and that would be *game over* for him! Unfortunately for Tom, occupied with these concerns, he neglected to notice a small hole in the ground coming up ahead. Just as he turned back to face forward, his foot dipped in the hollow and got caught. There was a thud and a brief utterance of a swear word as he found himself face down on the ground! Quick as a flash, Harry whipped past but not before Mia, seizing her chance, sprinted forth, cutting in front of Harry in a split second. Lily and Ijeoma followed closely behind, both gaining up in strides.

Then, just as the end of the track approached, something strange happened. The children began to sprint away from each other, away from the finish line itself!

Harry ran straight for the bench at the far right of the field whilst Tom, who had by now picked himself up in a scramble, raced towards the bin located ironically, close to their starting line. Lily dashed towards the lamp post and Ijeoma headed for the bollards in front of the Hospital.

By the time Mr Harold blew on his whistle signalling the end of the race, Mia was leaning against the abstract statue that stood in front of the Memorial Hospital and the others had stopped in front of their respective end points, all sweating and panting, breathless from the exertion.

"Great job guys!" clapped Mr Harold and waved them to come back. The children jogged back and crowded round him.

"That was a brilliant race!" said Mr Harold smiling broadly, "Now, can anyone tell me who won?"

The children looked at each other, unsure. Would that be Harry who had reached the bench first? Or was it Tom who ran the fastest?

Perhaps Mia who ran the furthest? Or Lily whose lamp post was the nearest to the track's finish line?

"Hmm," said Lily at last, "I'm not sure. Harry reached the bench first but Tom ran the fastest..."

"Although," Mia chimed in, "he *didn't* reach his finish post first..."

"Wait, but what about Mia," asked Ijeoma, "She ran the farthest, so shouldn't she be the winner?"

"What just happened there Mr Harold?" asked Lily, puzzled, "Why did everyone run off to different places?"

"Yeah," added Mia confusedly, "I don't understand. I thought we were all supposed to head for the statue."

"No," piped Harry, "I thought Mr Harold said the finish line was the bench!"

"Well," spoke Mr Harold grinning, "the finish line is actually *all* of those things - the lamp post, the bollards, the statue and so on - *for each of you*. What I did was tell each of you to head for it at the beginning of the race."

"But *why*?" asked Ijeoma. This was ridiculous. Why would Mr Harold ask each of them to race towards a different finish point?

"Yeah," agreed Mia, "now how on earth will we know who's won?"

"A-*HAH*!" grinned Mr Harold teetering dangerously over them, "that's the whole point!"

"I don't understand," replied Lily flabbergasted. "What kind of a race is this anyway?"

"It's the Race of Life," said Mr Harold sagaciously, looking very pleased with himself at the same time. With an exhausted oomph, he plonked himself on the bench.

"The Race of Life is exactly that," he continued. "You shouldn't compare yourself with other people. You see, you're all running a race but your destinations are very different."

He looked at Lily and continued, "So if you're busy checking out the person next to you instead of paying attention to your own running, you may stumble." Lily grinned sheepishly as she recalled looking at Ijeoma instead of concentrating on her own running earlier. Because of that, she had stumbled. Admittedly, there was some truth in that.

"Or," ventured Mr Harold, pausing and looking at Tom with a twinkle in his eye, "if you're always worrying and looking back, afraid that someone may overtake you, you may trip and fall." Tom rubbed his face a little sorely and nodded reluctantly.

"The point is," said Mr Harold looking round at the children, "don't compare yourself with others. When you're running a race, don't focus on the people ahead of you, beside you or even behind you. You might get disheartened if you compare yourself with the people ahead of you or you could get distracted by the people running beside or behind you. Run your best at your own pace because your finish line is different to everyone else's. The race you've just had represents life - and there is no winner or loser in life - because *your* finish line," said Mr Harold pointing at Lily, "is different to *his* finish line," he continued pointing at Harry, "...which in turn, is different to *her* finish line, see?" he concluded, pointing at Ijeoma.

"At school, it doesn't matter if you're not as good as someone else at something - say maths for example. You may be awful at maths but turn out to be a famous artist one day. You might not be good at science but you might grow up to be an amazing tennis player. You might decide you want to be a vet when you grow up, only to discover you're actually great at shoe design!" grinned Mr Harold.

"Whatever it is you do," he continued, "you should always try to beat *your* personal best, not others. Compare yourself with your previous performance, not someone else's."

The children nodded. It made sense. There they were comparing themselves earlier, wondering who was best at singing, who was better at music, who would get top marks in the exam when all along there was no need to - it didn't matter. And it didn't matter because there was no need to compare with each other. Everybody was different. Nobody was going to grow up to be exactly the same or do exactly the same things in life. So why would there be a need to excel in exactly the same thing as the next person? And what would be the point of comparing oneself with another?

"Or...," said Mr Harold with a wink, getting up to go back to class, "you might have thought you've always wanted to be a pilot, only to find out that - turns out teaching is a lot more exciting than flying after all!"

The New Girl

The Middle Way

We can always imagine more perfect
situations and how people should behave.
It is not our task to create the ideal. It is
our task to see how it is, to learn from the
world as it is.

THE NEW GIRL

"**I**t's the *new girl*!" announced Ijeoma excitedly, as she burst into the class-room, "She's *coming* this way!" The children crowded round her eager for details.

"How do you know?"asked Lily, clapping her hands, thrilled. New additions to the school, never mind their class, were always exciting stuff.

"I *saw* her," replied Ijeoma, eyes shining, "as I was coming out of the toilets!" She paused and added, "She's a little short for her age though..."

The children started chattering excitedly asking questions when Miss Duffy, their class teacher, stopped them.

"Now, now," she said calming them down, "back to your desks please." Everyone settled back down. But before Miss could address them, there was a little knock at the door.

Standing there was the school principal Miss Quinn and behind her, a smallish girl with curly, dark brown hair tied back in a pony tail.

"This is our new girl," said Miss Quinn, introducing her to Miss Duffy. Miss gave a smile and held out her hand to the girl.

"Hello Nadia," greeted Miss warmly, "my name is Miss Duffy." The girl didn't smile back. Instead, she kept her rather sullen look on and met Miss' handshake with a limp shake of her own. Undeterred, Miss ushered her to the front of the classroom and announced brightly, "Everyone, this is Nadia, your new classmate. I'm sure you will join me in welcoming Nadia

and making her feel at home here at St Ada's."
The class clapped and Frankie and Rocco
hollered "whoop whoop!" like a pair of enthu-
siastic gorillas before being instantly silenced
by Miss Duffy's disapproving glare. She then
directed Nadia to an empty seat next to Lily.

"Lily," said Miss, "Nadia will sit at your reading table. I want you to buddy up with her and
show her the ropes around here."

"Sure thing Miss, Aye-aye Miss!" answered
Lily with a quick salute, proud that she had
been selected to show the New Girl around.
Fancy being in the enviable position of getting
to know Nadia up close and personal before
anyone else in class!

Reading lesson flew by quickly and before
they knew it, it was over and time for lunch.

"C'mon Nadia," said Lily dragging a rather
reluctant Nadia with her towards the canteen,
"we have to hurry."

"Why?" replied Nadia, slightly sulkily, "It's
only break time. I don't see why we have to
hurry..."

"Because," cackled Lily rather enthusiastically, "this is when we *fight*!" Nadia's eyes
widened in alarm.

"Oh don't worry," continued Lily lightly,
sensing the other's trepidation, "we don't

really fight as such. You see, there's never quite enough space on the benches to sit down and eat as we share the same break-time as the Year Sixes. So us girls usually have to jostle hard and push the boys off if we want to sit together! Come on, I'll show you! Get your elbows ready!"

Lily moved Nadia along, down the corridor to join the usual bunch - Mia, Evie, Lizzy and Ijeoma - who were laughing and chattering excitedly as they made their way towards the canteen.

Lunch was a raucous affair - the canteen was already packed with children eating and talking excitedly, sitting elbow to elbow on the long, low benches at the tables. At the other end of the hall, the queue for school dinners bulged and shrank like a boa constrictor swallowing as children jostled in and out of their line, trying to cut in without attracting the attention of the very severe Miss Merola who presided over Lunch.

Miss Merola, who also happened to be the school librarian when not supervising lunch, was every inch her name. With her high collars, tweed skirts and ink-black cat-eye glasses, she hardly ever smiled unless it was to do with you following her 'Rules of Good Behaviour' such as walking in a quiet and orderly fashion, lining up in a perfectly straight line (no jostling) or sitting down and eating your dinner like a civilised adult (no talking with mouths full)... something which sadly unbeknownst to her even after all these years working at the school, was practically *impossible* for anyone below the age of twelve.

The girls made their way under her watchful eye to one of the tables with their trays after having acquired their lunches from the 'Demon Dinner Lady' as Lily nicknamed her.

"So have you any brothers or sisters Nadia?" asked Mia, shovelling her shepherds pie into her gob without so much as a chew. Like the Argos with a Thousand Eyes, Miss Merola raised a slow critical brow in Mia's direction whilst at the same time continued her unwavering gaze over a small group of decidedly over-excited Year Sixes by the water cooler.

Nadia shook her head in reply but didn't say anything. She was increasingly uncomfortable at the many questions directed at her whenever the opportunity arose for anyone to speak to her.

Ijeoma who had been sitting on her right, chatted excitedly to Lily about her birthday plans for the coming weekend. Lily in turn, was trying to convince her to include make up in the Pass the Parcel game. Having succeeded, she then turned to Nadia and asked, "So how old are you? I'm nine and Ijeoma's turning ten this weekend."

Nadia shrugged non-committally. Perhaps she didn't understand my question, Lily thought.

"*What year were you born then*?" asked Ijeoma, raising her voice above the din.

Caught unawares by Ijeoma's directness and insistence, Nadia answered her in a quiet tone, barely audible to the others. Ijeoma's eyes widened in surprise at the reply which Lily and the others didn't catch. But before she could say anything further, the bell went and all the children had to return their trays and line up to go back to class.

Later that afternoon, the girls found themselves congregated at the corner of the playground during second break.

"OMG, she's *eight*!" whispered Ijeoma conspiratorially to Lily, Evie, Lizzy and Mia.

"No *way*," said Lily, shocked, "That means she's a year younger than us! Is that even allowed?"

"Ssshhh! She's coming this way," hissed Evie spotting Nadia approaching. The girls abruptly stopped talking as she walked by but as soon as she had gone past, they huddled back together and continued chatting in excited whispers.

Nadia walked coolly across towards the other end of the playground and sat on one of the benches alone.

She had seen the girls gather round and heard their excited whispers, so she had pretended to walk past them casually in hope of being able to eavesdrop. Unfortunately stupid Evie had spotted her coming and was shushing them as she approached, so she couldn't catch what they were gossiping about. However she knew deep down, they were all talking about her.

I'll show them, she thought to herself, her cheeks flushing, I'll show them not to talk about me behind my back, these smug English girls!

"Guys," said Lily, noticing Nadia sitting alone on the bench, "C'mon, let's ask Nadia to play with us. She's new and she doesn't know anyone very well."

The others agreed and they all ran up to Nadia.

"Hello Nadia," greeted Lily, "do you want to play It with us?"

"Sure," shrugged Nadia carelessly as if it was no big deal.

The girls launched themselves into the game of It with gusto. In the beginning, there were lots of giggles and darting about.

"You're IT!" shouted Lily as she dodged Nadia's swipe at her and ran off laughing. She then doubled back as Nadia chased her and Evie. A rapid change in direction and tap! Evie was It! However that didn't last long as Evie did a nifty side step and promptly It-ed Nadia back!

"Not fair!" shouted Nadia back at the girls, her face darkening. She didn't like losing and started feeling hot and embarrassed.

"Well, don't get It-ed then, slow coach!"

teased Lizzy doing a silly wriggle before bolting past Nadia avoiding her outstretched arms.

Nadia stuck her tongue out only to be met with more laughs from Lizzy which only served to anger her more.

"I'm telling Miss!" she sulked and stomped off towards Miss Duffy to complain.

"Now what's the problem here?" asked Miss approaching them.

"Nothing Miss," replied Evie, "We were just playing."

"They keep It-ing me," whined Nadia.

"No we weren't," said Lily indignantly, "We were playing with you, silly. We were trying to be nice. Seriously, what is your problem?"

"Lily," interjected Miss Duffy sternly, "we don't talk like that." Lily bit her lip and kept silent.

"Now run along now all of you," continued Miss dismissing them, "Back to class now - break-time is over."

With dampened spirits, the girls disbanded and headed back to class.

Things continued to be difficult in the days that followed as the girls and Nadia tried to get along. Lily started to dread being Nadia's designated 'buddy' as it was becoming clear that that involved a mixture of trying to keep the peace between Nadia and the rest of the class, and giving in to Nadia's increasing demands for attention. Of late, the latter was becoming increasingly frequent and Lily was getting more and more complaints from her classmates for sticking up in Nadia's favour in attempt to keep peace.

"Lily," Tom said exasperatedly, "she's just threatened to tell Miss on me - and all because she says I didn't let her have another turn at the group 3D puzzle!"

Tom liked everything in an orderly fashion and acts of unruliness did not sit well with him - they had to be stamped out, like pimples that needed to be burst.

He continued, complaining earnestly, "That's not right! Everyone in our group has one turn each. Those are the rules. And now she's getting two, three turns. Can you *please* talk some sense into that girl?"

"Lily!" exclaimed Lizzy irritably, "she's gone and taken the gel pens from our table! For goodness sake, can you keep her in check please! And we want our pens back!"

Poor Lily. Inundated, she pulled Nadia aside to have a word.

"Nadia," said Lily, trying her best to explain, "you can't just do what you like - it's causing everyone lots of grief. The maths 3D puzzle for example - everyone at the table gets one go. Do you understand? One turn. You can't hog it for several turns as that'll mean the others won't get a go because we only have fifteen minutes to solve the challenge. See?"

"No," replied Nadia petulantly, "I don't."

"And these pens," continued Lily gruffly taking them from her, "they're the other table's. We can't take theirs - we have our own here..."

"But we don't have enough colours," Nadia replied stubbornly, "They don't even use these ones."

"No," Lily persisted, "we have to give these back. They're not ours."

"No!" cried Nadia and childishly grabbed the pens back from Lily, clutching them close to her. Like hyenas closing in for a kill, other children hovered nearby, sensing a standoff developing.

"*Give.. them.. back*," said Lily emphatically, firmly taking the pens off Nadia.

"Just take 'em off her, the spoilt child," goaded Lizzy, who had suddenly appeared behind Lily.

"Oh here we go again," moaned Tom, pulling a face at Nadia as he too crowded round, "Miss Bossy Boots taking over everything. Seriously, who do you think you are, coming into our school and lording over everyone like this?"

The crowd closed in. The air was filled with

a static belligerence that only nine year-olds who had had to put up with so much could muster. The mounting hostility was too much for Nadia.

"NOOOOOOOOOOO!" she wailed and ran off to Miss Duffy. Lizzy who by now had had enough and couldn't care less, stuck her tongue out after Nadia whilst Evie shook her fist angrily towards her.

"Oh man..," groaned Lily as they all watched Nadia in front of the classroom, all teary and pointing at them to Miss, "this is not good..."

Miss Duffy beckoned sternly at them to come to the front of the classroom.

"This behaviour is not to be tolerated," she said disapprovingly, "Lily, Tom, Evie and Lizzy - go to Miss Quinn's office now please. This is not how we behave in class."

So the four made their way reluctantly to the headmistress' office.

Miss Quinn was a very successful headmistress with a personality to match - modern, outgoing and efficient, she had a certain peppiness about her and a presence which commanded attention and respect from children and adults alike. Children would just as easily hug her at the end of term as they would cower if they were being told off for misbehaving. One of the more forward-looking members of her profession, Miss Quinn had somehow managed to be strict but approachable at the same time and children were not only unafraid to make their case if they felt it was so justified but even encouraged to speak their minds. However this time, the children weren't quite sure which side of her they were to encounter - the strict or the approachable - it was literally a precarious toss-up between the two as they nervously entered her office.

"Ah!" said Miss Quinn looking up from her sleek Macbook as they came in, "Lily, Tom, Lizzy and Evie. Come in and close the door behind you." Tom meekly closed the door and they all stood tentatively in front of her desk.

Miss Quinn's office epitomised the spirit of the school. Modern and individualistic, it was painted in a cool shade of blue-grey with a few comfortable chairs covered in soothing sandy coloured fabric. Several tall vases of colourful, sprightly snapdragons and lilies provided vibrant bursts of colour amidst the neat oak desk, the meticulously tidy shelves of books, a few hung paintings and the odd school photograph - all reflective of Miss Quinn's exacting nature.

"Now," began Miss Quinn, bright but business-like, "I understand there have been... difficulties in Nadia fitting in class and all of you getting along, the latest culminating in the episode at class just now. Can someone tell me what happened?"

Compelled by the fact that she was Nadia's buddy, Lily reluctantly spoke up, recounting what had happened at class - Nadia taking the other table's gel pens and not letting others at her table have a go at the maths puzzle. The other children nodded, agreeing, as she carried on, adding in their various accounts of the situation every now and again. Miss Quinn listened patiently without interrupting.

"And," finished Lizzy hotly, "apparently she's *eight*! Should she be in our class?"

"Also," Evie added, "I don't think she's Catholic, Miss Quinn - at RE lesson, she didn't know what we were talking about. Should she even be in our school?"

When they had all finished saying what they had to say, Miss Quinn paused for a moment thinking deeply and then spoke, "Firstly, I'd like to explain to you the criteria for being accepted at this school. As a Catholic school, places are firstly offered to Catholic children who have an older sibling already at this school. Then, remaining places are offered to Catholic children living closest to the school, followed by children from other Christian denominations. This is then followed by children of other faiths."

She paused for a minute and then continued, "An opening came up in your year due to Sophie's departure from our school last term. If you had an older brother or sister at this school, you would be first to be considered for the place. If there were no one else on the waiting list for this opening that met the criteria I explained earlier, then any child of any faith would be considered for the place. Now this happened to be the case and Nadia happened to move to the UK at the time and applied for a place in our school - that's how she gained a place here. Do you know where Nadia is from?"

The children shook their heads.

"Nadia is from a country called Iran which unfortunately does not treat its citizens very well, especially those of faiths different to the Muslim faith. Some of its people who have converted to Christianity have even been threatened with death. So as you can see, it can't have been a very easy life there for Nadia and her family. As a result, they have had to leave their country and come here for their own safety."

"Oh," said Evie, "that explains why she's never heard of Teen Sing or Swim - makes sense now."

"Yeah," nodded Lizzy, "she said the other day that she's never watched telly before! Fancy that!"

Miss Quinn smiled a little as it began to dawn on the children that Nadia came from quite a different set of experiences to them and that it would be quite impossible to expect her to behave and talk in the same way as they did right from the start. In fact, it was also very likely that she didn't understand some of the everyday things they did and the very things they had in daily life that they took forgranted.

"As Christians," continued Miss Quinn in her well-modulated voice, "we must be kind and help those in need *regardless* of what religion they belong to. Whether or not Nadia is Catholic, Christian, Muslim or of no religion, she deserves our help and love just as much as any of you. This is why our school have offered her a place when we could, and this is why we have to be patient with her and help her get used to life here at St Ada's. Will you children try to help her now that you have an inkling of what it's like to be in her shoes?"

The children nodded to show they understood, Lily perhaps less enthusiastically than the others at the thought of her role as Nadia's buddy. Then with a curt nod, the children were dismissed to return to their class.

✳ ✳ ✳

It was Home time and as the bell rang, the children poured out of their classrooms into the playground, eager to fit a few last precious minutes of play before being taken home by their waiting parents.

Evie ran up to Lily, giving her a friendly pat on the back.

"You're It!" she taunted mischievously. Lily laughed and chased her round the playground, roping in Lizzy along the way. It wasn't long before Ijeoma and Mia joined in and soon all of them were tagging each other in their favourite game of It.

Some of the mums stood by watching. As was customary, they would wait around in the playground chatting with each other, letting their children play a bit until Miss Merola, who on gate duty (when not on lunch duty or library duty) would announce, often after a fairly long time past home-time, that the gates were closing and Didn't-everyone-have-homes-to-go-to?

Nadia stood by tentatively, with a look eager to join in. Lily noticed and darted by, playfully tapping her on the shoulder yelling "You're It!". Nadia ran after her and the others, trying to get them. A few rounds of various people getting It-ed ensued much to the delight of the girls.

"Is that the new girl Nadia?" asked Lily's mum looking on.

"Yes, I believe so," replied Evie's mum,

"Miss Beckett mentioned she's from another country."

"Ah..," came the reply.

"Iran, I've been told - by one of the teaching assistants," Mia's mum chimed in.

"Migrant circumstances I heard," said Evie's mum, "Can't be easy on the kid. I hope our children are helping her find her feet here."

"They seem to be okay from the looks of things," noted Tom's mum.

"Aye, you say that," replied Evie's mum, "apparently Evie's been telling me they've been having tiffs with this Nadia."

"Yes," joined in Ben's mum, "I've heard that as well. I don't think some of our kids have been very nice to her. That's not right and I think they could be ganging up on this poor girl."

As if on cue, the mums looked towards their brood playing only to find Lily and Evie shaking their heads and telling Nadia they didn't think she should play It with them anymore. Nadia turned away, red faced and ran off, tears streaming down her cheeks.

"*Lily Tripitaka!*" called Lily's mum sternly, "Come here this instant!"

Lily looked up, startled at the tone of voice and walked up to her mother. Evie's mum also called Evie over.

"Why were you excluding your friend from your games?"asked Lily's mum accusatively.

"But Mum...," started Lily, trying to explain, "She was getting annoyed again so we thought it best that she stopped playing with us...before she starts complaining again."

"She gets like this and we just don't want any more drama from her, see?" added Evie hotly.

"*What*?" said Evie's mother shocked. "You don't treat people like that - it's not proper like. I did not raise you to be a mean girl Evie McLoughlin!"

"But Ma...!"

"You girls are simply ganging up on that poor girl," continued Lily's mum. "This not acceptable and counts as bullying. I cannot believe I'm seeing this sort of behaviour from you Lily. Go and apologise to your friend now please."

"But..!" protested Lily and Evie fervidly.

"No buts! *Go*," ordered Evie's mum, giving the girls a very stern look.

Reluctantly the two girls shuffled towards Nadia and mumbled some words of apology before returning to their mums to go home.

Nadia said nothing but stared after them, her eyes agleam with a soft glow of triumph and with the slightest hint of sly smugness curled at the corner of her mouth.

The weeks passed by and lessons came and went. There were days when Nadia did not cause any trouble for the rest of the children but sadly these were few and far between.

Lily was by now used to her sudden outbursts of tears and various other attention seeking tactics. It was beginning to grate on her and there seemed no end to the special concessions Nadia enjoyed that Miss would never *ever* in a million years let anyone else in the class get away with. Lily felt jealous and resentful. It was grossly unfair and she hated Nadia now more than ever.

Lugging her heavy bag across the playground at Home time, Lily ran towards her mum who was waiting to pick her up.

"You all right Bee?" asked Mum, calling her by her pet name. Bee was short for baby, simply because Lily was always her baby and the baby of the family.

"Aaargh, horrid, *horrid* girl," muttered Lily angrily, "I'm so fed up with her!"

"Whom?"

"This Nadia," replied Lily throwing her bag onto the ground in frustration, "Mummy, she is so *annoying* - I *hate* her! Why can't she just be nice? Why does she have to always cause trouble for me and the other girls! *Oooh*! I've really had it with her!"

"Now Lily," coaxed her mum, "Remember we talked about this before. You need to cut her some slack - she's new here."

"She's not *that* new Mum," Lily replied irritated, "She's been here for months and months already - next week is practically the end of the school year. And she's *still* the same Nadia - she still threatens to tell Miss on us if we don't do what she wants, she still gets away with all sorts of things in class without getting a yellow card and she's always chatting the teacher up. What makes her so special she gets all this attention and special treatment? To top it all, she's still the troublemaker she was from the first day we set eyes on her. I so can't stand her! Aaarghh!"

"Well," her mum continued, "have you ever thought about why she gets under your skin? Makes you so angry?"

"Er 'cos she's *annoying*?" came the reply loaded with sarcasm.

"Well, sometimes the reason someone repulses you is because you and that person have more in common than you care to admit. That person wouldn't get to you if you didn't have anything in common - it wouldn't rile you as much see?"

"I don't see what I could possibly have in

common with *her*!" replied Lily glaring wrathfully towards Nadia who was standing beside Miss along with the other children waiting to be collected.

"Perhaps," suggested Mum, "it could be that you're jealous she's getting all this attention and special treatment from teachers. That could be a reason." Lily pulled a face at Mum's observation - Mum knew she was the jealous type.

"Another reason could be because you see part of yourself in that person - you recognise the flaws in her you don't like which deep down, you could be guilty of too if you were in the same situation," continued Mum.

Lily shrugged impatiently as if to show her disagreement but Mum continued ignoring her daughter's passive repudiation, "For example - forcing others to do what you want - I can see that's possibly something *you* might do if you didn't have the discipline to check yourself and stop yourself from acting that out."

Lily opened her mouth to protest but closed it again, silent. She had to admit - there was some truth in what Mum said. It was certainly true that part of her intense dislike for Nadia came from her jealousy at the attention Nadia received and she had to admit too that the thought of Nadia bullying her and her friends into giving in to her repelled her immensely. And that was because she saw herself possibly guilty of that in the past and didn't like the feeling that thought gave her.

"We can always imagine more perfect situations and how people should behave," explained Mum gently, "however, it is not our task to create the ideal. It is our task to see things as they are and to learn from the world as it is."

"Look," she said, nudging Lily. Lily looked in the direction Mum was looking at. A youngish man in his early twenties came to pick Nadia home.

"That must be her uncle," Lily told her mum. "Nadia said her uncle picks her up usually."

Mum stared after them - the man flicked the last of his cigarette over the fence and into the school playground. Then, much to the annoyance of Miss Merola on gate duty, exhaled the acrid smoke in front of her and waved Nadia over impatiently. Nadia started after him, laboriously lugging her oversized schoolbag and trying to keep up. Turning on his heel, he walked off, not caring to look behind to check if she was following him or not.

"Be kind, Lily," said Mum thoughtfully, "Even if you can't bring yourself to like someone, that's fine but don't be mean or unkind, ok? People may have problems we don't know about."

"Yeah, but..," Lily started to protest impatiently. Mum staggered a bit but Lily caught her in time.

"You ok, Mummy?" she asked a little worried. Mum had been having her fainting spells again lately and had been to the doctor's last week for another checkup.

"I'm tired, Lily," Mum replied, "Let's go home, shall we?"

Lily smiled and nodded, holding her mummy's hand. They walked home slowly. It was summer and next week was the last week of school before they broke for the holidays.

'Thank goodness,' thought Lily, 'I've just about had enough of drama with Nadia this year and I'm so looking forward to the holidays and starting Year 5 in September'. She cheered up considerably at the thought of the long holidays to come. Things looked brighter already. But little did she know how wrong she was...

Things take a Turn for the Worse

The Truth of Suffering

"I wish it need not have happened in my time," said Frodo.
"So do I," said Gandalf, "and so do all who live to see such
times. But that is not for them to decide. All we have to
decide is what to do with the time that is given us."
- JRR Tolkien, The Fellowship of the Ring

THINGS TAKE A TURN FOR THE WORSE

L ily and Leah were sitting at the breakfast table. It was the last day of school for both of them but for Leah, it was all the more poignant as it was also the last day at the school both she and Lily went to, for she would be starting secondary school elsewhere in the autumn.

"So what're you bringing for Toy Day today?" asked Leah, munching her toast slightly distractedly.

The last day of school was always Toy Day which meant no work and children were allowed to bring in toys to play with.

Lily shrugged, "Nothing much, just some pots of slime."

"Still trying to sell your home-made slime eh?" sniggered Leah, "Have you even made back the money you spent buying the glue and borax in the first place?"

Lily paid little heed to her sister's remark, retorting sardonically, "SOOO glad I don't have to put up with *you* in the same school next year..."

Leah simply sniggered, brushing off the comment and continued eating her toast unperturbed.

"Wonder what's taking Mum and Dad so long this morning?" asked Lily.

It was half eight already and they were meant to have left the house ten minutes ago. As usual, Mum would drop them at school whilst Dad went off to work. It wasn't like them to be late.

"Mum! Dad! Time to go!" Lily hollered.

Quietness followed, in which could be heard the sound of the neighbour's dog barking from beyond the garden, and then the sound of footsteps coming down the stairs.

A moment later Dad came into the room followed by Mum. She looked tired and pale, and there were circles under her eyes which were slightly red as if she had been crying. Dad had a sombre expression on his face as both he and Mum sat down at the table.

"Your mum and I have something to tell you," said Dad. His voice was quiet, flat almost - not giving away anything. Lily wondered if this had anything to do with Mum - Mum had been having her fainting spells again but surely no more than usual? Perhaps she was tired. At any rate, she and Dad had been going to the hospital for checks in the last few weeks.

"Mummy is not very well at the moment and she and I will have to go to the hospital more frequently in the coming weeks. Your grandma will come and stay with us to help out more - take you Lily, to school, pick you up and cook dinner for all of us. Leah will take the bus on her own as she's old enough to do so now. Mummy will need lots of rest at home and Lily, you can't play with her as much okay?"

Lily nodded meekly, looking at him, and then at Mum.

"Are.. are you ok Mum?" she asked plaintively.

She didn't understand fully what was going on, except that there was now a knot of uneasiness growing in the pit of her stomach and an unspoken anxiety amongst them all in the room.

"Yes Bee," nodded Mummy, trying to sound cheerful. Her voice cracked a little. She patted Lily affectionately on the head and murmured, "I just need to rest more and I'll be fine." Then she reached out her hand towards Leah and hugged both girls.

* * *

The summer weeks marched on and Mum's hospital trips came and went with a blur. As it was still summer holidays for the girls, Grandma stayed with them to help out when Dad went to work or when he had to take Mum to the hospital.

Lily didn't like having Grandma around. Short and slightly on the plump side, Grandma in her seventies, was a bit doddery and completely out of touch with anything remotely current.

Having her live with them most days during the week meant the constant blare of the telly in the background, streaming episode after tedious episode of the Antiques Rummage or reruns of Friends For Supper, all of which were slowly driving Lily insane. Grandma also hadn't the faintest idea whatsoever of what children of Lily's age were into, so unfortunately for Lily, her idea of a fun afternoon involved dragging Lily to the park to play on the kiddie swings and slides amongst the toddlers and preschoolers.

Leah on the other hand, avoided all this by assuming the persona of the typical teenager and holing herself up in her room, not talking to anyone.

'I swear there's something she's not telling me,' Lily thought to herself irritably, 'It's almost as if she's avoiding me so as not to have to talk to me or risk me asking her something. But *what* is it? What *is* she hiding??'

And so this was how the weeks passed - interminably for Lily, enveloped in this feeling of unspoken tension and uneasiness in the house.

❊ ❊ ❊

One afternoon, Lily crept quietly to Mum's bedroom, listened at the door, then nudged it open a little to look in. Mummy slept most of the time these days, especially after the hospital visits.

"Hey Bee," said Mummy faintly as she noticed Lily's head poking through. Lily tiptoed in and slid into Mummy's bed for a cuddle.

"Is it ok if I huggle you for a bit Mummy?" she whispered as she laid her head softly on Mummy's chest.

"Of course," replied Mummy stroking her hair, smiling a little.

Lily looked up at her and reached out her hand to stroke Mummy's soft hair in return. To her horror, she found herself holding several clumps of Mummy's hair.

"Mummy, what is this?" Lily stuttered, her face paled at the sight.

Mummy looked down at the clumps of hair and said nothing. Hearing no answer, Lily glanced up, only to see tears streaming down her mum's face.

"Don't cry Mummy," cried Lily, who started crying herself, "Please don't cry! I'm sorry Mummy, I'm *sorry*! I didn't mean to..."

"Shh," comforted Mummy. "It's okay, it's not your fault. It's just hair. I'm fine."

She brushed her tears off quickly and gave Lily a hug. "I love you Bee," she whispered, holding her tight.

"I love you too Mummy," replied Lily tears streaming down her cheeks, "And I'd *still* love you even if you didn't have any hair."

Mummy gave a little laugh. "I think we'll get the hairdresser in tomorrow, shall we? I'm going to get a trim. You can get your hair done too if you like."

Lily nodded and snuggled Mummy briefly before tiptoeing out again to let her sleep.

❉ ❉ ❉

"What is going on Leah?" demanded Lily as she burst into Leah's room.

Leah looked up from her book and unhooked her headphones.

"What?" she asked, pausing the music track.

"*What's going on*?" repeated Lily looking at her in the eye, "With Mum. And don't lie to me Leah."

"I don't know what you're talking about, Moody Face," replied Leah, pulling a face.

"I'm talking about THIS!" said Lily, holding out a clump of Mummy's hair in the palm of her hand, almost shouting in frustration. Her eyes glistened with anger and exasperation.

"THIS, Leah! **THIS**! This bloomin' *thing* which nobody seems to want to tell me about!" cried Lily. Her voice broke towards the end.

Leah took one look at the hair in Lily's hand and her face drained of colour. She sat down on her bed speechless, her expression drawn and white.

"Mum has cancer," she said, almost in a whisper, as if afraid that if she said it out loud it would take the shape of the reality she was denying to herself all this time. "She's been having chemo - chemotherapy. That's what the hospital visits have been. Dad's been taking her for chemotherapy sessions. She's very, very ill Lily."

"What..," asked Lily hesitantly, "what does that mean?"

Leah remained silent.

"Leah..?" begged Lily, tears streaming down her cheeks. The knot that had sat in her stomach all this time twisted even more.

"It means she could die!" burst out Leah, sobbing uncontrollably.

Lily's heart sank to the pit of her stomach and she felt her limbs turn to mush as the seriousness of the situation crashed over her like a wave, squeezing every last bit of breath out of her.

"No,"she wept, *No!* and hugged her sister. They clung desperately to each other, like two helpless little buoys adrift in a vast, turbulent ocean. Outside Leah's bedroom window, dark clouds were gathering. It was as if to echo their predicament, an ominous storm from which there was no escape was approaching, threatening to engulf them.

✳ ✳ ✳

The next day saw the arrival of Mrs Shah the mobile hairdresser, to the house.

The girls vaguely remembered her. They had only ever seen Mrs Shah perhaps once or twice before, when they were very little, for Mum had used her to cut their hair when they were too young to be easily corralled into the local salon.

Leah who was growing her hair long, had politely turned down the offer of a haircut and had retreated to her room.

Lily however told Mum she wanted one after Mum had had hers done.

Mrs Shah hummed a lively Hindi number as she busily snipped away in Lily's room whilst Mum relaxed in her chair admiring her new pixie cut.

"There," announced Mrs Shah appearing at the doorway, "all done Mrs Tripitaka."

Lily emerged from behind her. Mum took one look and started to cry.

"Oh Bee," she half whispered, reaching out and hugging Lily. "Why did you do that? You loved your hair - you've always wanted to grow it long."

She knew that Lily, being a girly girl, loved having long hair. It was always a tussle trying to get her to keep hers at bob length as Lily always wanted it longer which would have swamped her delicate features. At any rate, Lily's bob was now no more - she had hers cut short like a boy's.

"I prefer it like this Mummy," she replied softly, wiping Mummy's tears away. "Now we can both have the same hairstyle."

It wasn't long before the heat of summer soon gave way to the cooler temperament of autumn.

There was a feeling of change in the air and an undercurrent of melancholy echoed the change in the colours of the surroundings. The falling leaves and even the smell of the air around all signalled the end of summer with its brash heat and heralded the beginning of autumn with its apprehensive coolness.

School had started. However this time, to Lily it felt different - daunting even, for Leah was now at a different school, having started her secondary education. To top it all, Leah was currently away in Rome on a school trip for a whole week. The house felt even emptier and quieter than usual.

Grandma dropped her off at the school gate. Lily waved her off and walked glumly to class.

School no longer felt fun anymore. It was

just one long tedious day after another until the weekend when she was at least free from Grandma and her endless television programmes before it started all over again on Monday.

Even the girls at school weren't any better, Lily thought irritably to herself: 'There she goes again - Lizzy showing something off to the girls - probably some new Scenty pencils, or some stupid pencil case or another. Predictable little twit. Ijeoma's just as bad, the shallow cow she is - prancing around with a new hairdo every other week. I see she's got beads weaved into her braids this time - in the colours of Chelsea apparently. Classy...*not*! Uugghh!' Lily kicked the legs of her desk in annoyance.

"*Lily!*" snapped Miss Tyron, their new Year 5 teacher, who looked and sounded every inch of her name, "Yellow card - for kicking the table and being a general nuisance."

Lily stood up abruptly, making her chair slide back with a harsh screak, causing Tom and Evie nearby to cover their ears in dismay, then sauntered airily across the room to change her card.

"Sometime today would be nice Lily," continued Miss Tyron testily.

Lily rolled her eyes at the remark which unfortunately for her, was noticed and infuriated Miss even more.

"Make that a *Red* card then," fumed Miss.

Lily gave a careless shrug and changed her card before sauntering back to her seat, defiant as ever.

Break time couldn't come soon enough. Despite having to stay in because of her red card, Miss Tyron let her out slightly earlier so she could join the rest of the class in the playground.

Lily walked up towards the girls. Evie, Ijeoma, Lizzy, Nadia and Mia were crowding round the water cooler. They were talking and laughing. Evie was telling them about her weekend at Go Gorrilla with her parents.

Go Gorrilla was an outdoor activity place where you could climb across rope bridges on tree tops and zip-wire your way through.

"Lily, this one's yours," said Evie, thrusting a little toy gorilla into Lily's hands, "I went to Go Gorrilla during the weekend with me dad and mum - Oh my goodness, it was so *fun!*"

"We've each got one," chattered Lizzy, waving her soft toy gaily, "Look - Nadia's has purple eyelashes!"

"So was it scary Evie? Being so high up?" asked Mia.

"Nah," replied Evie self-assuredly, "but my mum was *terrified*! We were in the middle of this rope bridge and she decided to look down..."

The girls giggled.

"So of course she froze with fear," continued Evie, laughing, "and wouldn't budge one bit! Dad had to come all the way round to get her. It was hilarious!"

The girls were giggling at the image of Evie's mum stuck, shrieking amidst the treetops when Lily cut in saying, "What a wuss your mum is. Fancy being afraid of heights - how *stupid* is that!"

The girls stopped laughing and looked at her gobsmacked. This wasn't the first time Lily had been mean. Ever since school started again, it was as if she had turned from her usual kind, chirpy self into this completely different, horrid, rude person. There wasn't a day that passed without Lily getting into trouble at class either or lashing out at one of them and no matter what they did to try and be nice to her, it made no difference whatsoever. It seemed as though they were target practice for her, there to bear the brunt of every mean word and action she could throw at them.

"How can you say that," said Evie, choking back her tears and bitterly snatching the toy back from Lily. Lizzy comforted her as she furiously wiped her tears away.

"Don't take it to heart," said Ijeoma giving Lily an indignant glare, "she's just *jealous*."

"Oh Lily, why'd you have to ruin things again? You're *hopeless*!" sighed Mia exasperated.

They all walked away from Lily, leaving her behind, standing alone in the playground.

"Well, the HELL WITH YOU TOO!" yelled Lily after them and stomped off red-eyed, in the opposite direction towards the benches.

A little while afterwards, Nadia found Lily sitting all by herself on the bench at the corner of the playground, vehemently making scratch marks on the seat with a sharp twig. She looked up and scowled as she saw Nadia approach.

"What do you want?" she asked rudely as Nadia came and sat next to her.

"Nothing," came the soft reply.

"*Weirdo*," responded Lily and continued to scrape at the wooden bench with her stick.

Nadia hesitated a moment, then took out her toy gorilla and handed it to Lily.

"Take it," she said, as if she didn't hear Lily's words. "If you hit it like this," she continued, punching her fist into the squidgy toy, "it feels good."

Lily looked at her and said nothing. Then she punched the toy several times, hard. It did feel good. She gave a small half-suppressed chuckle. Nadia gave a little snicker herself and they both continued to sit there - Lily squeezing the toy and Nadia sitting next to her. Both said nothing - words were not needed. It was as if an unspoken understanding had somehow burgeoned between them.

After a while Nadia spoke up, "You know, they're trying to help you - your friends."

"Yeah..."

"They just don't know how because you always push them away."

"I know. But I can't help it…"

"I know."

"Yeah."

"It's ok."

Lily shifted a bit, then continued, "I guess you know what it's like huh? To be the most despised person in class…"

Nadia shrugged, "It's ok."

Lily glanced at her. Who would've thought - never in a million years did she imagine that the one person whom she disliked the most turned out to be the *only* one that understood her, the only one that really *got* her.

She started telling Nadia about mum and her illness, about the sickening feeling in the pit of her stomach all the time and the intense anger - so much anger - that she felt constantly.

Nadia in turn, told her about her life before and how different it was, how she missed playing freely outdoors like she used to, how cramped it was living here in London, how money was tight and so on.

As the girls exchanged their secrets, they also shared their hopes and fears with each other.

"So why did you always tell on us to get us

into trouble?" asked Lily.

"To get attention of course," replied Nadia matter-of-factly. Lily's eyebrow lifted questioningly.

Nadia explained, "No one pays me any attention at home - I'm nobody. I'm invisible. At most, I'm just the inconvenient extra mouth to feed."

Lily looked at her thoughtfully. What a strange answer! And yet, she kind of understood. She had seen how Nadia's uncle and indeed her father's off-hand manner with Nadia at drop off and pickups. It must be awful to be treated like nothing - like nobody. Lily couldn't imagine what it would be like, for even with her and Leah, they were very much an important part of the family. It was unthinkable to imagine a scenario where they didn't matter one bit and it was shocking to think that in Nadia's family, the family car was, as she revealed, much more important to them than Nadia herself!

"I found that I could get people's attention if I cried or went to the teacher," Nadia continued. "And I liked that. So I started doing that every time I felt insecure."

"Yes, but didn't you realise that made us all *so* angry with you?"

Nadia shrugged, "At least you weren't *ignor-*

ing me."

"Oh," said Lily.

"Oh," came the reply.

And then the bell rang for classes to resume. Lily got up to walk back to class.

"I'll see you back in class," Nadia said hurriedly and rushed off the other way.

Lily gave a shrug and continued on, unaware that Nadia had gone to speak with the other girls, to tell them why Lily had been behaving the way she had all these weeks. After a brief discussion amongst themselves, they made their way back to class, looking for Lily, planning to give her a big hug and to tell her that she had them to turn to no matter what.

"Lily!" Evie called out, "Wait up!"

Lily turned round. However, just as the girls were running up towards her, Miss Whitfield from the office popped her head at the door.

"Lily," she said urgently, "there's a telephone call for you in the office. Please can you come now, quickly."

Lily nodded and followed her into the office. The other girls gestured at her to tell her they'd see her back at class.

Miss Whitfield shut the office door and handed the receiver to Lily.

"Hello? Hello? I can't hear you very well,

Dad," said Lily straining at the telephone.

"Let me put it on speakerphone," said Miss Whitfield help-fully, sensing Lily's frustration and pressed the speaker button.

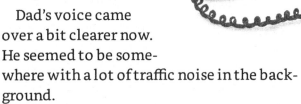

Dad's voice came over a bit clearer now. He seemed to be some-where with a lot of traffic noise in the background.

"Lily," Dad said hurriedly.

There was a tone of urgency in his voice, "Something's come up and I can't pick you from school today. Grandma will come round, okay?"

"I don't understand Dad, aren't we going swimming after school?" asked Lily.

She could hear the sound of sirens in the background, getting louder and louder.

"No, no, we can't," replied Dad sounding flus-tered, "I,.. honey! *Honey!*"

"Mum? *Mum*? Is Mum with you??"

There was a commotion in the background.

"Sir, *sir*, I need you to stand back," someone was saying urgently.

There was a lot of shuffling noises in the

background and Lily could hear Dad calling Mum repeatedly.

"Dad!" cried Lily, her heart thumping wildly, "what's happening? *What's happening*??"

"I'm in the ambulance with Mum," replied Dad breathlessly, "it's going to be okay. I'll talk to you lat... *honey*!! Oh no, no no, *honey*!!!"

A flurry of commotion and activity in the background obscured Dad's voice.

"*Mum*? MUM??" shouted Lily as the line went all buzzy, "no WAIT!" Then a click. The phone went dead. Lily screamed.

"She's dying! She's DYING! Please.. *please...*," she cried wildly, tears running down her cheeks, "I want my MUMMY! I WANT MY MUMMY-YYY!!!"

She flung herself against Miss Whitfield who hugged her tight as she convulsed into a heap, sobbing uncontrollably.

Home time that day felt surreal. Lily was very subdued when Grandma came to collect her. They returned home in silence.

Grandma too, had not heard back from Dad since the afternoon so it was an anxious wait for them as they both tried to get on with their daily routine as best they could. Leah was still in Rome on her school trip so the house was eerily quiet and empty.

That night, Grandma made soup for dinner but neither were hungry. Lily barely ate at all and Grandma hadn't the heart to make her.

"Will Mummy be home tonight, Grandma?" asked Lily when bedtime approached. She was frightened - the house was so empty without Mummy, Daddy and Leah. And she couldn't imagine going to bed at night without Mummy tucking her in.

"No, Lily," answered Grandma gently, "I don't think so. Mummy is in hospital and your Daddy will be with her tonight."

As Grandma closed the bedroom door behind her, Lily curled up in the corner of her bed, feeling more alone than ever, hugging her legs close to her chest, tears slowly soaking into her pillow.

At about midnight, the phone rang. It was Dad. He said Mum was in intensive care and they were monitoring her. He then told Lily that he would be staying overnight at the hospital and Grandma was to drop her off at school tomorrow. Lily nodded meekly before finally putting the phone down.

An Unexpected Ally

The Ever Changing Nature of Things

Love is the absence of judgement
- Dalai Lama

AN UNEXPECTED ALLY

T he days that followed passed slowly like a hazy dream, and not a good one. Leah had returned from her trip which Lily was at least thankful for.

A routine soon formed within the household - Grandma would drop Lily off at school in the mornings, Leah being older, would take a bus to hers and Dad would commute by tube to his office in the City. When school was over, Grandma would pick Lily up, whereas Leah would get back on her own. Dad usually reached home later as he would visit Mum at the hospital after work.

The girls ate their dinner with Grandma. Dad often had his late and would then retreat into the study to work some more 'til the wee hours of the morning. They hardly saw Dad apart from the rare occasion when he happened to dine with them.

Money was tight now because Dad was now the sole earner of the family with Mum no longer able to work. Takeaways during the weekends, eating out or buying treats were now a thing of the past. Grandma cooked and they all ate in all day, everyday, to save money. Lily hadn't appreciated those little luxuries they had had in the past until now.

School was at least, slightly better. The girls rallied round Lily and despite the occasional 'grumpy' episodes from her, there were generally less tiffs and she didn't seem to incur the wrath of Miss Tyron as much as she used to.

*　*　*

It was still fairly sunny that afternoon when Lily and Leah strolled to Green Cottage to collect their takeaway.

Grandma had given them some money for that night's dinner as she was tired of cooking all week and wanted a rest.

"It's been *ages* since we've been here," commented Lily as the familiar smells of roast duck assailed their nostrils.

"Heavenly," sniffed Leah, ravenous, "I miss their roast duck.."

"...and sweet sour chicken balls.." added Lily.

"...and kailan..."continued Leah, giving Lily a wry smile.

"...and *salt and chilli pepper squid*!" they both exclaimed in unison, laughing, as they entered the takeaway.

"Hallo hallo," greeted Uncle who was standing at the counter, "Long time no see!"

"Hello Uncle," greeted the girls.

"Where's Aunty?" asked Lily.

She had never seen Uncle at the 'Position of Authority' behind the counter where the cashier stood. It was always Aunty who manned it so it struck Lily as particularly odd to see Uncle there instead.

"Oh," replied Uncle, "out in the backyard, praying."

"Praying?" queried Lily, nosy as ever.

"Yes," explained Uncle patiently, "Praying. It's the Hungry Ghost festival. You know *Hungry Ghost festival*?"

The girls shook their heads.

"It's a Chinese tradition where we honour the ones who have passed away," explained Uncle. "A bit like the Spanish and their Los Muertos - Day of the Dead. Can you see Aunty in the back courtyard lighting joss sticks and placing food out as offerings?"

Lily and Leah strained their necks to look. Leah being slightly taller of the two could just about make out Aunty bowing deeply several times, clutching a bunch of smoking joss sticks in her hand. Lily couldn't see much but sniffed at the heady scent of sandalwood and incense drifting in from the back garden.

"Is she praying to God?" Lily asked.

Leah elbowed her to shut up and not pry. However Uncle gave a faint smile and answered, "She's probably offering prayers to her parents, her grandparents,... and our son."

"Your son? You have a *son*?" said Lily, surprised.

"*Had*," whispered Leah nudging her sister not to probe any further.

However Uncle didn't appear to mind or notice and murmured, "Yes, our son - Chin Yung. We lost him,... it would be forty-one years ago now. He fell ill you see."

The girls flinched at the reply. Lily's eyes reddened. Uncle saw that she was clearly upset and added kindly," It's ok Ni Ni - it was a very long time ago." He glanced up towards the back garden where Aunty was still praying and then softly added, "But don't bring it up when Aunty comes in, ok? She still finds it hard after all these years."

Lily's eyes welled up and tears now flowed freely down her cheeks in rivulets.

"Ni Ni, what's the matter?" asked Uncle concerned, as her tears dissolved into sobs.

"Our mum is very ill," explained Leah. "We're very, very worried."

"Ah," said Uncle, his brows furrowed.

"*I don't want her to die* Uncle!" Lily burst out in anguish. "I will be a good girl from now on. I will be good forever - for *life*,... if only God will make her better! I promise! I *promise* with all my heart!"

Uncle looked at her, his old eyes brimming with compassion and understanding that could only have come from himself knowing how she felt.

"Yes, Ni Ni. I know what it's like to want something so badly, so desperately," he said quietly. "But we have no control over these things Ni Ni."

"But she *can't* die, I won't let it! I *won't*!" cried Lily clinging desperately to her sister. Tears flowed down Leah's cheeks as she held her little sister close.

Leah looked at Uncle, her eyes glistened and said, "I *wish* mum never had cancer. I just wish we could wake up from this awful living nightmare."

Uncle gave a heavy sigh and sat down slowly on his little stool, rasping his fingers together as he usually did whenever he was thinking deeply.

"Have you heard of Kisa Gautami?" he asked.

The girls shook their heads.

"Long ago," Uncle started, "when Buddha was still alive, there was a woman called Kisa Gautami. She had a little baby boy, her only son.

However not long after, her son fell ill and died. Kisa was heartbroken and carried the dead child around the village begging people to help her. At last one of the villagers asked her to go to Buddha for help.

When she told Buddha her sad story, he listened and then said to her, 'There is a way to solve your problem. Go and find me some mustard seeds. However these seeds must come from a family in which there has never been a death.'

Filled with hope, Kisa went from house to house asking for some mustard seeds.

At the first house, a woman offered to give her some mustard seeds. But when Kisa asked if she ever lost a family member to death, the woman said her grandmother died a few months ago. So Kisa turned her down, explaining why she could not take those seeds.

Next, Kisa visited the home of another person. However the woman was a widow - her husband had died a few years ago. Once more, Kisa could not take those seeds as they didn't meet Buddha's requirements.

Kisa went onto another house but again, someone had died - this time an aunt.

And so on and on Kisa went, from house to house, but each and every time the answer was the same - every house had lost someone to death."

Uncle looked up as he finished his story.

"Do you know what the story was trying to say?" he asked gently.

Leah nodded, followed by Lily, reluctantly. Like Kisa, they had come to realise that there was no one in the world who had never lost a family member to death. Death was very much a part of life no matter how hard they wished it didn't exist.

"Life, sickness, old age, death...," said Uncle, "They are all part of our existence whether we like it or not." He sighed and continued, "That is the Truth of Suffering. It exists - no point trying to avoid it or refuse to accept it . You cannot control it. And you can't bargain with God either, even if you believe in one."

Then he looked up and looked at Lily squarely in the eye.

"Ni Ni, do you remember when you were worried about your exams and we practised mindfulness through archery?"

Lily nodded.

"Remember the danger of letting fear take over? Whilst we have to accept that illness and death exist, remember that at the moment, your fear of losing your mummy is just that - the feeling of fear. We don't know what will happen and that is something that is out of our control. The only thing you can do is concentrate on the present moment. Do what you can to help your family and each other. Take things one day at a time and leave the rest. That is what you must do."

Uncle patted Lily's head tenderly, "It will be difficult, I know and not always possible to keep at all the time. But you are both very brave girls and you will be able to go through this difficult time. It will be hard but understand that this too shall pass because nothing stays the same forever. That is the way of things."

At that moment, Aunty came into the shop, slamming the back door behind her and dusting a bit of ash off her sleeves.

"Ah hallo girls," she said, "Lee Lee - come to collect your loast duck ah?"

Lily nods.

"Hello Aunty," greeted Leah.

"I'm very sorry for your loss!" Lily blurted out.

Leah shot her an alarmed glare. Aunty started a little, gave Lily a slightly quizzical look before registering a look of realisation a split second later.

She then answered softly, "It's ok Lee Lee. It was not meant to be." Then she gave Uncle a gentle squeeze on the arm before disappearing into the kitchen to retrieve the girls' order.

"Nah, here you go, girls," said Aunty appearing with a bag containing a stack of boxes of piping hot food.

"Thank you Aunty," said Lily.

"Thank you Aunty," echoed Leah, slightly apologetically.

Aunty smiled at both of them, something she very rarely did, and then produced an exquisite red rose freshly cut from the back garden and handed it to Lily.

"May you too," said Aunty tenderly as she bade the girls goodbye, "always find beauty in life no matter what life throws at you."

Christmas is Coming

Death and Rebirth

My sun sets to rise again
- Robert Browning

CHRISTMAS IS COMING

The days melded into weeks and the weeks into months. Breakfast, school, dinner, bedtime. The girls soldiered on. Grandma helped with the household chores and Dad worked relentlessly. Mum was still in hospital.

Leah completed her Eleven Plus exams with flying colours and Lily's little 'business' of selling slime to her friends at school was making her enough pocket money to buy takeaway dinners for the family every Saturday so that Grandma didn't have to cook.

Then one morning, as the girls sat down to breakfast, Dad came down and announced, "Would you two like to see Mummy today after school and maybe start thinking about helping her pack?"

The girls looked at Daddy excitedly. He nodded, smiling for the first time in a long, long while.

"She's coming home?" asked Lily, her heart swelling in hope.

"Yes, the doctor's given her the all clear and

she can finally come home," Dad answered.

"Mummy's better!! SHE'S COMING HOME!!!" yelled Lily jumping up and down, tearing round the kitchen like a lunatic and grabbing Dad, Leah and Grandma excitedly.

"She'll be home for Christmas," Dad said, "but she still needs lots of peace and quiet to rest, is that clear?"

The girls nodded excitedly. They were over the moon - Mum would be back home by Christmas!

That evening, after visiting Mum, Lily and Leah walked to the Green Cottage to collect some dinner.

"Orr-dorr *pease*!" snapped Aunty behind the counter, brisk and business-like as usual.

"Hello Aunty," greeted Lily smiling for the first time in a long, long time. "We've come to collect - under the name Tripitaka please."

Aunty looked up, glanced up and down at her and said, "Your order coming Lee Lee. Wait here - five minutes ok?"

Lily nodded. Aunty didn't say anything further but disappeared into the back kitchen with the faintest hint of a smile at the corner of her thin lips.

"How are you Ni Ni?" came a familiar voice from behind the counter.

It was Uncle, sitting low on his stool watching his tiny telly again. With a grunt, he stood up stiffly, his tanned, bald head emerging over the counter like a smooth, brown spaceship. She gave him a friendly nod and replied cheerfully, "Good."

"Oh, like that ah?" replied Uncle, twinkle in his eye, looking from one sister to the other.

"Mummy's going to be home for Christmas," Lily said excitedly, "The doctor's given her the all clear. I'm so happy - I can't wait!"

"That's wonderful news!" exclaimed Uncle, overjoyed.

"I know..," replied Lily, "I was so scared before. I was so afraid she would die."

"What happens when we die, Uncle?" asked Leah suddenly, very serious.

"Well," said Uncle thoughtfully, "nobody really knows. Although, Buddhists believe that death is just another change in a series of never ending changes."

"A *change*?" asked Lily, incredulously.

Leah shuddered. "Well the thought of dying frightens me," she said. "Ever since Mum fell ill, I'd been thinking about it. Imagine not being able to be with the people you love anymore. And what if where we go after death isn't ...nice?"

"Ah," murmured Uncle, "you've hit the nail on the head. People are afraid of death mostly because of one of two reasons. The first is fear of the unknown - what happens to us when we die? Will it hurt? Will it be dark? Will it be scary?"

Leah nodded.

"I should hate it if it were dark," she agreed.

"And if I stop breathing when I die," added Lily, " ...and I know that because they always do that breath test to see if someone's dead ,...will it be painful?"

Uncle chuckled.

"I don't think it'll be painful - you would have gone beyond all physical sensations by that time I think. Anyway, that would probably be the least of your worries at that point," he said good-naturedly.

Then he continued, "The second reason why most people fear death is attachment - our attachment to the ones we love, our possessions or our sense of self - what makes you, you. Will I never see my mother again, my father, my sister, brother, my beloved dog, cat or hamster? Will I never be able to live in my beautiful house again? Will I no longer be 'Me' when I die?"

Lily nodded wholeheartedly.

"I couldn't bear the thought of never seeing Mummy again," she whispered solemnly, "it was too painful."

Leah sighed, "To think we're going to have to go through all of this in the future again when Mum and Dad are ninety." She shook her head, depressed at the thought.

"Well," said Uncle, "they'll be back again, in another form. Buddhists believe in rebirth."

"What do you mean?" asked Leah.

"Like zombies?" queried Lily, a little doubtfully.

"Ha ha!" laughed Uncle. "No, not like zombies Ni Ni. Ha haha, good one!" He looked down behind the counter and began rummaging in a drawer there.

"Buddhists believe that when we die, we simply change form," continued Uncle, throwing out an odd assortment of objects - a rubber plug, a screwdriver, a small plastic Pokemon figurine - as he continued his search for something.

"We are constantly changing. Just like water which evaporates, becomes a cloud, turns to rain, forms rivers and becomes part of the ocean, so do we when we die - we change form and the cycle repea... *Hah*! Found it!" said Uncle, triumphantly clutching a rather varied bunch of candles, having rifled through the entire contents of the drawer.

"Whaa?" asked Lily, puzzled but intrigued at the same time. Uncle always did and said the most unexpected things.

"*This*," said Uncle standing a row of candles up in a straight line on the counter, "is *rebirth*!"

It was a peculiar mix - five candles each completely different to the other - some tall, some thick, some thin, some tiny, all different in colour, shape and size.

"Huh?" said Leah, looking on quizzically.

"People always think that rebirth is when the soul moves from one body to another body - like the movie Ghost! You know the movie *Ghost*? With Patrick Swayze - very handsome, but dead now, shame. So good looking - Aunty's favourite actor..."

Uncle hummed the theme song from the movie, momentarily lost in his recollection of it.

"Um, Uncle?" prompted Lily, amused.

"Ah? Oh yes," continued Uncle, snapping back to the present. "Rebirth is not reincarnation - *not the same*! You understand? *Not* like the movies where the soul floats from one body into the next. Rebirth is *change*, like the flame of this candle." At that point, Uncle lit the first candle on the counter.

"Oooh, pretty," remarked Lily, her eyes transfixed at the flickering flame dancing in front of her.

Uncle cleared his throat, like a professor about to deliver a very important lesson, and continued pointing at the first candle, "Imagine this candle is your body. The candle and its flame together make up you - the person. Buddhists believe that when we die, like the flame, we move to another candle - another body." Then Uncle lifted the first burning candle, transferred its flame to the next candle and then blew out the first candle, putting it back in its place at the front of the line.

"See?" he said pointing at the second candle which was now burning next to the extinguished first candle. "The flame from the first candle now burns on the second candle. Is it the same flame? In a way, yes - because it came from the first candle, but in other ways No, because this flame now burns off a different candle which is made of different wax, different colour, different chemical composition. So you could say it is, in a way, a different flame."

Next, he took the second candle and transferred its flame to the third candle and blew out the second candle. The same was repeated until the flame had been transferred to the final candle, leaving the other extinguished and slightly smoking candles behind.

"See?" Uncle said, "*Rebirth*! The flame goes on and on and on forever. But it also never stops changing. You are not the same person you were in your previous life. This is what rebirth is believed to be like."

"Hmmm," commented Leah with a chuckle, "I wouldn't like to be that short, ugly candle if I can help it."

"Ha ha ha," laughed Uncle, "well that depends on your karma. What that means is, if you've been good in this life, you'll be reborn into a better life. Buddhists believe that if you have been bad in this life, you could be reborn in a less fortunate form or even as an animal in your next life."

"I dunno," said Lily unconvinced, "how do we even know if all this is true? What if when we die, that's *it*? Like, that's really it - no rebirth, nothing. I mean, who says for sure we're coming back to this earth anyway?"

"Good point!" answered Uncle. "Well, you're here right now aren't you? So even if you don't believe in Buddhism, you believe in science and maths don't you? So if you were born and you exist here on earth, now, there is therefore a mathematical probability that this could happen again as it's obviously happened once already."

Then he added, his face breaking into his comical, toothy grin, "...but preferably not reborn as a chicken."

"Why not chicken?" asked Leah as she collected their takeaway and the two sisters made their way towards the exit.

"Because everybody likes *to eat* chicken!" replied Uncle with a guffaw.

All You Need is Love

Loving Kindness

This is my simple religion. There is no
need for temples; no need for complicated
philosophy. Our own brain, our own
heart is our temple; the philosophy is
kindness - Dalai Lama

ALL YOU NEED IS LOVE

"**D**o you think we should invite Uncle and Aunty from Green Cottage to the party?" asked Lily, busily cutting out bunting for Mum's homecoming party.

"Why not," commented Leah, breathing stentoriously through her mouth as she laboured on stringing the bunting provided by her sister and trying not to let her runny nose trickle too much in the process. "They've helped us a lot and besides, they might even bring some roast duck to our party."

"Good idea," agreed Lily grinning mischievously. "I *like* the way you're thinking. I'm going to pop over to the takeaway to drop them an invitation."

Lily hurried up with her cutting, shoving the last stack of triangles at Leah with an impish chuckle. The girls laughed, carefree laughs, the type they had not known for a long time, playfully throwing scraps of material at each other. Mummy was coming home!

Everyone was busy with preparations for

the party to welcome her back - Grandma ensconced in the kitchen busy cooking and baking, Leah and Lily creating decorations and invitations, Dad setting up them karaoke system and everyone making cards and presents. This was going to be the best Christmas-Homecoming party of the century!

The day of the party finally arrived. It was on the weekend before Christmas and school had just broken up for December holidays. Grandma had cooked enough food to feed an army and the house looked festive and colourful with strung up bunting, fairy lights and a big, satin streamer with the words "WELCOME HOME MUMMY" in big letters over the front door.

Lily and Leah had invited some of their classmates, their parents, Mr Harold, family friends and of course Aunty and Uncle from Green Cottage. The house was bursting with people and music was thumping merrily from the karaoke speakers.

The car pulled up at the door. Lily could hardly contain her excitement - out stepped Mummy with Daddy helping her. She looked radiant and happy. Lily and Leah ran and flung themselves on her.

"Mummy! Mummy!" exclaimed Lily as she hugged Mummy hard.

Tears rolled down Mummy's cheeks - she was so happy to see the girls. Lily held onto her hand, not wanting to let go - it was unbelievably wonderful to have Mummy back home and have her kiss and tuck her in tonight!

By now the party was getting into full swing. Lily looked around for her friends. Harry, Evie, Tom and Lizzy were talking animatedly in the corner. Lizzy was wearing an amazing full length frock of pale pink with a slightly iridescent chiffon layer floating delicately over it.

'WOWWW,' gaped Lily, 'That is one amaaazing dress. It must have cost a small fortune to look like the Oscars. I wonder how she's going to keep it clean and pristine?' As if on cue, Lizzy looked down at her dress, fingering it gingerly to check she hadn't smudged anything on it by accident.

'Hmm,' chuckled Lily to herself, 'much too high maintenance for me...'

She then moved her gaze onto Harry who was standing next to Lizzy. Ah, Harry....

Lily gulped and looked at her own outfit. Grandma had surprised her and Leah with their early Christmas presents that morning. Unfortunately for Lily, hers was a horrifically loud Christmas knitted jumper with the largest, most *inaccurate* knitted design of Disney's Rapunzel in it, which Grandma had insisted she wear to the party.

'Oh heck,' she thought to herself, 'How on *earth* can I talk to Harry looking like *this*?'

Then Lily heard her name called above the music. Uncle was waving at her cheerily. She weaved her way over to him, taking pains to stay out of Harry's line of sight and holding her tray of nibbles up high in order to hide as much of her jumper from sight as possible, just in case he looked her way.

"Wonderful partee Ni Ni," said Uncle, raising his glass as Lily came round and offered him some dainty Chinese lettuce wraps.

"Are those your friends?" he asked pointing at Ijeoma, Ella and Nadia who were having turns singing at the karaoke. Lily nodded.

"Who's the shorter girl - the one with curly dark hair?" asked Uncle interestedly, indicating at one of the girls who had pulled a sulky face and stamped her feet. The others next to her shifted uncomfortably and there was a sense that they were going to have to give in to the sulky one if they didn't want her to cause a scene.

"Oh that's Nadia," answered Lily looking on rather nonplussed, "Looks like she's not happy it's someone else's turn with the microphone."

"Ah - *Nadia*," nodded Uncle, who by now knew most of Lily's friends through her vivid accounts of events at school.

"Looks like she may be back to her ol' self," shrugged Lily, chuckling.

Uncle grinned and nodded approvingly at Lily.

"A few months ago, you would have been so frustrated at her slipping back to her old self, but now..," he continued, "you are Zen! *Zazen*! Peaceful! *Very good*!"

Lily laughed, amused and said, "It is not for us to create the ideal..."

"...but our task to see how it is, and to learn from the world as it is," finished Uncle, nodding approvingly. "You have learnt well my grass-hopper," he chuckled.

Both of them looked on, observing the girls as one would observe passers by from a cafe. Then a surprising thing happened - when Ella grudgingly handed Nadia the microphone, Nadia refused it and handed it back to Ella with a grin.

"*Wow*," said Lily, surprised, "I did *not* see that coming. She's stopped making a fuss for a change!"

"Hah!" chuckled Uncle, "people can change for the better too, if they so choose to." Lily smiled as she watched the girls continue singing merrily on the karaoke.

"Well, Ni Ni," murmured Uncle thoughtfully, "We've learnt a lot this year haven't we? I certainly have - the truth of suffering, karma, wisdom and compassion, impermanence, mindfulness... "

" Uncle," asked Lily, "amongst everything you've just mentioned, what do you think is the most important lesson of all?"

Uncle smiled and said without hesitation, "Love and kindness."

The doorbell rang again - more and more guests were arriving. Lily caught her breath as Mia swanned in looking gorgeous as ever. From the corner of her eye, she spied Harry straighten up at her dramatic entrance and felt a pang of jealousy as he left his group to go up to talk to her.

"Lily!" hollered Lizzy, temporarily bringing her back from her thoughts on Harry, "Come sing with us!" she pleaded.

"Also...," yelled Evie waving madly, "I need more slime - new ones!"

Lily nodded. Grinning broadly, she set her

tray down and reached for her ever ready stock of slime kept in the sideboard. Not one to miss a sale, she excused herself from Uncle and hurried over with it.

"Which ones do you want?" she asked, opening a huge container full of little plastic pots of slime in every colour imaginable, "Strawberry Milkshake? Jiggly Jade? Butter Slime?"

"Or..,"she continued, opening one labelled Special, and slid out a fluffy blob of lilac goo with pride, "*This* - my latest creation - *Cloud Slime!*"

"Ooooooo," cooed Evie and Lizzy together, taken in by the incredible fluffiness of texture the latest creation offered.

"I *want*!" declared Evie, "Lizzy - this one even matches your dress!"

"WOAAH, not so near!" said Lizzy inching back quickly, afraid the slime would get on her dress.

"Oh c'mon Lizzy, stop fussing about your dress and have some fun," teased Evie.

Lizzy shook her head, checking her dress again for the umpteenth time. This was getting exhausting, she thought to herself.

"If you're not careful," quipped Lily as if reading her mind, "that dress of yours is going to become a burden. It's called attachment - Uncle told me. You don't want to get too attached to things. It's gonna be a right ol' pain if you do."

Lizzy thought about it and seemed to come to a decision. She nodded and then pointed at one of the pots of slime.

"I like this one - Jiggly Jungle Juice. Can I have it?" she asked grinning and reaching into her dainty slingbag.

"Sure. One pound fifty."

"Deal."

Lily stuffed the money down her jeans pocket and handed Lizzy the pot with its bright green contents.

"Er, hi. Can I buy one too?" came a voice from behind.

Lily turned to see who it was, only to see Harry standing behind her, shuffling his feet a little uncertainly.

UGLY JUMPER!

"Er," replied Lily, swiftly holding up the box of slimes in front of her hideous jumper, "Sure. Which one do you want?"

"Hmmm," said Harry, looking carefully at the varied selection before him.

"This one," he said, pointing at a buttercup yellow one.

"Good choice," said Lily approvingly, "my personal favourite - Butter Slime."

Harry smiled a little sheepishly and held out some cash.

"Thanks Lily," he murmured little shyly.

A brief pause and then a hurried stutter: "I really like your slimes."

Lily looked at him and smiled. For some strange reason that made Harry blush.

"I also like your slimes much more than Mia," he blurted out quickly, turning bright red and then hurried off clutching his purchase. Now it was Lily's turn to blush.

"Maybe it's the jumper that did the trick," chuckled Ijeoma, suddenly appearing at her elbow, along with Nadia and Ella.

Lily groaned.

"It's my Christmas present from Grandma," she explained, "She *made* me wear it especially for this party." Looking down at her jumper she continued, "I don't even know *what* Disney princess this is supposed to be!"

The girls peered closely.

"Hmm," ventured Ijeoma, "looks like Rapunzel I think, but the hair's not quite long enough..."

"It's quite possibly the most revolting Christmas jumper I've ever seen," chuckled Ella.

"Yeah," agreed Ijeoma.

"Oh yeah," grinned Evie and Lizzy in unison, there and then cementing Lily's top firmly in

166

the World's Most Hideous Jumper category.

"I think my mum knitted that," piped Nadia suddenly, looking at the jumper more closely. The girls stopped short and looked at her.

"What???" said Lily.

"Yeah," continued Nadia, nodding firmly, "I believe my mum knitted this. Look - she always knits the face like this and this is the coloured wool she always uses for hair. You can't mistake it - it's like an artist's mark although er.., in this case I don't think we're talking about anything artistic! Well, you know what I mean...."

"Seriously...?" said Lily, groaning further. You just couldn't make this up. The girls burst into hysterical laughter.

"Yup," chuckled Nadia, affirming, "I'm sure now. You see, my mum volunteers at the local Persian Cultural Centre on the High Road nearby. She often knits scarves and jumpers for the charity to sell."

"That would explain it," said Lily, slapping her forehead with a groan, "Grandma says she often goes there after dropping me off at school to have a coffee. That explains a *lot*!"

Lily went on to tell them that in addition to the jumpers she and Leah received that morning, Grandma also got Dad a shisha pipe for

Christmas. The children burst out laughing at the thought of Grandma doing all her Christmas shopping at the Centre.

"Oh my gosh," said Evie wiping off her tears, "that's the funniest thing I've ever heard."

"And that's still the *ugliest* jumper I've ever seen," giggled Lizzy.

Lily laughed too, shrugging her shoulders in resignation.

"Although...," piped Ella suddenly, "It kinda looks like Harry Heartthrob if you look at it from here, don't you think?"

"Oooo, you're right Ella, it does!"

"Hahaha, so it does!"

"Aw *cool*! It does look like Harry Heartthrob from Pop Royale!"

"Haha! It actually looks pretty cool if you look at it like that!"

And just like that, the children decided it wasn't such a bad jumper after all.

The arresting bars of the French national anthem 'La Marseillaise', followed by three long notes singing '*Love - love - love*' blared from the speakers, rousing everyone in the room.

"I *love* this song!" exclaimed Mia's mum, slapping her thighs in rhythm as the tambourines picked up the steady beat of the Beatles' song: *All You Need is Love.*

"Flippin' fantastic song this!" agreed Evie's mum getting to her feet and moving to the beat.

The song picked up, gathering more people to their feet as it steadily progressed towards the chorus.

"*Nothing you can do, but you can learn,*" sang Ella's mum passionately at the top of her lungs.

"*How to be you in time,*" bellowed Ijeoma's dad

in a surprisingly musical bass tone.

"*It's easy...,*" belted Evie and Mia's mums in harmony.

Then the entire room let loose with the chorus:

"*ALL YOU NEED IS LOVE...!*" sang everyone at the top of their lungs, "*ALL YOU NEED IS LOVE...! ALL YOU NEED IS LOVE, LOVE... LOVE IS ALL YOU NEED...*"

The children sang along at the top of their voices, arms linked around each other, swaying to the music. Grandma grabbed Mr Harold for a dance as he clung on his crutches for dear life, twirling on it like a spinning top. At the other end of the room, Evie's Dad swept Nadia's mum up in a lively jig and Lily spotted Lizzy's mum bringing Aunty another drink. Dad was twirling Mum on the dance floor and Mia and Tom's mums were weaving in and out of the crowd, serving canapes and chatting. All the people who had helped and supported each other in some way, big or small. All the little kindnesses, all the connections, all bound by love.

"Love and kindness," mouthed Lily to Uncle who was sitting across the room, merrily tapping his feet to the music. He nodded, his protruding front teeth flashing like a pair of gigantic headlights as he beamed. She had finally understood.

When the song finished, they all crowded round for a group photo.

"Closer! Closer!" urged Ijeoma's Dad, motioning the girls to bunch up closer together to fit into the shot, "You guys look grrreat! This is going to be *the perfect shot*! Ready..., one..., two..., three..., CHEEEESE!"

The Preferably-to-be-Read-with-an-Adult Bit...

THE PREFERABLY-

TO-BE-READ-WITH-AN-ADULT BIT

PHEW! What a rollercoaster ride Lily's had, don't you think? From mean girls to helping the homeless, to drama, life and death. Do you sometimes think life's a bit like a rollercoaster? If so, you're pretty much SPOT ON!

Like Lily, we're constantly on life's rollercoaster, riding its ups and downs. We are over the moon when life is great. For example, It's the school holidays! And it's my birthday! I'm having my best mates over! We're going paint-balling! Then the cinema! And we're having a party! Life is Awesome!! But we feel sad when good things come to an end (My birthday's over! Why did the party end so quickly? I wish we could go paintballing again! I have nothing left to look forward to! Life Sucks!!!). We get upset when things go wrong (I didn't make it to the swimming team! I'm a failure!) and when they haven't gone wrong, we worry about them going wrong anyway (I'm going screw up my trials! I'm never going to make the swim team!) We want what we don't have (why don't I have a million dollars?) and we refuse to accept things that we haven't a choice on (I'd give a million dollars not to have to sit that exam!)

However, like Lily, there is a way to look at these challenges differently and there is a way to not feel angry, upset or scared. From understanding why some-times people are mean towards  you (such as in the chapter *Oww That Hurt* where Lily discovers that everything has a reason and the reasons have their reasons) to the ever changing nature of things (where Nadia, the girl Lily hates the most, turns out to be her one true friend), there is a way to handle these nasty mishaps that life tends to throw our way.

So, what is it? What's the secret to being able to tackle anything and everything that life can possibly throw at you?

Well, as with all things it's probably best to start at the beginning...

❃ ❃ ❃

Buddhism is a way of life (adults like to use big words and call it a Philosophy but that just means a way of life). The same way science provides us with a way of explaining how things work, Buddhist teachings provide us with a way of making sense of the world around us and a way of explaining the suffering in our lives and around us.

Buddhist practices train us to see things as they are, without being clouded by our personal intentions, our own selfish feelings or desires. This allows us to see things more clearly, make better decisions and do the right thing.

Funnily enough, 'doing the right thing' in Buddhism doesn't always mean being good. Unlike the movies, in Buddhism there is no good or bad, no right or wrong. Buddhists believe in whether an action is skilful or not skilful. Skilful means to look at a problem impartially (meaning without being influenced by personal intentions or desires) and then take actions to produce the best possible result to end suffering.

So how did these Buddhist practices come to be? They came from the teachings of a man

called Buddha who worked this out for himself a long time ago.

Now most people refer to Buddha as the bloke who came up with the teachings of Buddhism - that person's real name was Siddharta Gautama and he was a prince who was born in Lumbini (now Nepal) at about 483 BCE.

However Buddha is actually a title, not a name. It means 'One Who is Awake'. Siddharta became the first Buddha through his years of study and meditation.

It all started when he was about 29 years old. As a prince, he lived a sheltered life and one of luxury. He was even married with a son! The story goes that one day, he saw an old man by the roadside, then a sick person and after that a dead body. It then struck him that ageing, sickness and death were an inescapable part of life. This affected him deeply - rich, poor, young or old, man or woman - everyone would inevitably age, fall sick and die. Was there an alternative to just accepting the realities of old age, disease and death? Was there a way out of all this suffering or were WE ALL DOOMED??

He then spotted a wandering mendicant (that's basically someone who belongs to a religious order, who doesn't own anything and

survives off alms from people) and decided to leave his life as a prince and live as a wandering ascetic himself to search for truth and liberation from suffering. (An ascetic is someone who lives a very simple life for religious reasons, giving up all pleasures and luxuries of life).

After years of searching, trial and error (at one point, he nearly died from starvation having gone to the extremes of self-deprivation), Buddha found the way out of suffering - the *Middle Way* - and became Enlightened (meaning he basically sussed it out).

Buddha then spent the rest of his life dedicated to sharing this knowledge and teaching the principles of Buddhism (called *Dharma*, meaning Truth) with the aim to bring an end to suffering and share in the happiness, wisdom, peace and *Nirvana* that he himself discovered. *Nirvana* is a state of perfect peace, where there is no suffering, desire or self, where one is free from the cycle of death and rebirth.

The basics of Buddha's teachings are contained in what's called the Four Noble Truths. Just as the basics of maths are covered by the four basic operations: addition, subtraction, multiplication and division, the basics of Buddhism are covered by these four principles. The Four Noble Truths are :

* The Truth of Suffering (1st Noble Truth)

* The Origin of Suffering (2nd Noble Truth)

* The Truth of Cessation (3rd Noble Truth)

* The Truth of the Path (4th Noble Truth)

The next few sections give us a simple description of each of these Truths and using examples from Lily's adventures, show us what they actually mean.

Finally, the most important message of Buddhism is that in order to attain enlightenment, your attitude to life must be that of great compassion, meaning be kind and help others. Only when you are kind and selfless will you be able to see things clearly, allowing you to open your mind and through practice, develop it and shape how you live.

THE FIRST NOBLE TRUTH : THE TRUTH OF SUFFERING

The First Noble Truth is the Truth of Suffering which states that suffering (also called *dukkha*) exists. Yes, it's a bummer but suffering such as birth, illness, ageing and death are an inescapable part of life. Additionally, suffering like loneliness, fear, frustration, anger, disappointment, jealousy and sadness also exist.

The First Noble Truth teaches us to understand that all this suffering exists and to accept this fact. You cannot escape suffering - it is real and there is no point in trying to avoid or deny it. For

example, in *Examination Woes*, Lily wishes exams never existed. She suffers stress and worry because deep down, she refuses to face the fact that exams exist - she keeps wishing they didn't. How often have we heard someone say, "Oh, how I wish I wasn't so unlucky" or "If only this didn't happen to me"? The truth is we've all had things happen to us that we wish didn't.

However, like Lily and her exams, we have to accept that misfortunes or challenges like that can and do happen. Instead of asking, "Why me?", the question we should be asking ourselves is *what do we do* about it? Uncle advises her to accept this fact of life and when she does, the tension of 'fighting' or denying this fact goes away, leaving her to concentrate on how to handle her fear of failure and tackle the problem.

There are also other types of *Dukkha* such as suffering due to the ever changing nature of things and suffering due to the impermanence of things (meaning nothing stays the same forever). In *Examination Woes,* Lily wishes her dreaded piano exam were as easy as her previous one. She gets stressed and suffers because she refuses to accept that nothing ever stays the same. But things are ever changing. In this case, she cannot expect exams to always be easy. As in life, things are sometimes easy, sometimes hard.

Similarly in *Things Take a Turn for the Worse,* Lily wishes that her mum never fell sick. This is one of the hardest challenges faced by our heroine and Uncle advises her to accept that things change in life, sometimes for the worse and are unfortunately out of our control so that she isn't wasting her energy fighting this fact, but instead to try and take things one day at a time and help where she can with the things she has control of.

Lizzy's beautiful frock in the chapter *All You Need is Love,* is a source of happiness (or so she thinks) but ends up being a burden to keep clean and causes her frustration and unhappiness instead. This is an example of the ever changing nature of things. Sometimes the things we think will bring us happiness may change and end up bringing us unhappiness instead. Even the photo finish at the end of the story where Ijeoma accidentally spills the slime shows that things don't stay perfect forever.

 And along the same line of things always changing, in *An Unexpected Ally*, Nadia - once Lily's arch enemy - turns out to be her friend and supporter, demonstrating that it's not just events that constantly change but people as well.

Lastly in full circle, at the end of *Examination Woes,* Aunty cheekily reminds Lily that there will be more exams to come in the near future - a reminder of the Truth of Suffering: that suffering exists and there will invariably be more challenges to come. But fear not, the next few Noble Truths will give us an idea of how we can overcome these challenges!

THE SECOND NOBLE TRUTH : THE ORIGIN OF SUFFERING

The Second Noble Truth tells us about the origin of suffering - where does suffering come from? Now that we understand that suffering such as sickness, ageing, death and impermanence exist, what is it that actually causes this suffering? What causes us to feel pain, anger, jealousy, disappointment, sadness, frustration and so on?

The Second Noble Truth tells us that the root of our suffering is our ignorance. We are ignorant of the laws of causality (also known as *karma*), the ultimate nature of reality and of our desires and attachments. This is why we suffer.

For example, in *Oww That Hurt,* Lily suffered anger and bitterness towards Evie because she was ignorant of karma. She didn't realise that events that happened previously led up to Evie hitting her with the eraser. This is the law of causality, also known as *karma,* meaning things happen as a result of other things. In life, we often blame our misfortunes on other people or 'on society'. We think in terms of black and white

- she hit me and therefore it's her fault. We think that that's all there is. It isn't and that's not how you should look at things. Often we don't realise that these 'misfortunes' are the result of past actions. We then go on to be attached to the bad emotions we feel (called *klesha*) such as anger or hate. This encourages us to blame others for our misfortunes instead of seeing the issue for what it actually is - a result of past actions. In this chapter, Lily actually finds out about the past actions that led up to Evie hitting her and in fact one of them was that of Ella trying to shield her from being hit at Dodgeball.

To gain victory over our *kleshas*, we must first find a way to contain any negative actions that may come out as a result of these - meaning don't let our feelings result in us doing or saying something harmful in return. For example, Lily should refrain from negative actions such as hitting Evie back or saying something hurtful back.

The next step as Uncle says, is to tackle the root of the problem. So for example when someone broke the window at the takeaway, Uncle had the police arrest the vandal to teach him a lesson and to prevent further occurrences of violence and destruction.

And finally, we must root out any remaining

negative feelings left within us. Uncle tells Lily to "Remove it! Let it Go!", meaning forget about it, don't hang onto the anger. The inner enemy at the end of the day is ourselves!

In *Joe Bordeaux*, Evie and Ijeoma suffer frustration. Their suffering is caused by their desires or wants - they *want* Joe to act a certain way, to be a certain way.

In this case, they want him to be sensible with the money Evie's given him, they want him to be responsible and take good care of the coat and shoes that  Ijeoma obtained for him. This is a very common type of desire most of us are unwittingly guilty of. We *want* people to conform to our expectations, we *want* people to behave a certain way, we *want* others to like us, we *want*. All these are examples of desire - of wanting. But this is not the reality of things (if Joe was by nature sensible with money and responsible with his things in the first place, he wouldn't be a homeless person!) It would be unreasonable to expect someone to be something they're not. Uncle on the other hand has the wisdom to see the problem for what it is and suggests a better solution for it which is to put Joe in touch with the charity that helps him find his feet.

The gameshow that the girls watched with Uncle also illustrates the importance of having wisdom as well as compassion. Compassion means concern for the suffering of others. It teaches us that compassion needs to go hand in hand with wisdom in order to be effective. However compassion is vital and in my humble opinion, even if one is not wise, it is important that we should be at least be compassionate! Compassion is *really* important as there isn't enough of it in the world as it is today.

In *The Luckiest Girl* the girls suffer the unhappiness, frustration and jealousy of not getting what they want - to be the prettiest, the richest, the most popu-

lar etc. The story is a good example of why most of us experience these feelings and it is due to us desiring things. If we give up these desires we will be free from suffering. As the girls find out, the moment they relinquish their desires (to be the prettiest, most popular etc), they find happiness within.

Sometimes one can be attached to bad emotions too. In *Examination Woes*, Lily becomes attached to her fear and lets that take control over her. She lets the fear of failure become a reality to her when in actual fact she hasn't failed - she was just *afraid* that she would fail. The solution to the problem was to free herself from her attachment to the emotion Fear. We often don't realise that strong emotions arise from assuming the reality of something that is unreal. Lily thought so much about her fear of failure that it became a reality to her - she forgot her fear was a feeling and unwittingly believed that she would actually fail. The Third Noble Truth tells us that all this suffering can be overcome.

THE THIRD NOBLE TRUTH : SUFFERING CAN BE OVERCOME

* (Also a great song, by Queen!)

Well, after all the doom and gloom about having to face the 'facts of life' as it were, the good news about the Third Noble Truth is that suffering can be overcome and happiness and contentment is possible (YAY!). The Third Noble Truth basically says that if we give up our desires and attachments we will be free from suffering. To do this, we need to see things for what they really are.

In the chapter *Oww That Hurt*, Lily was upset when Evie hit her with the eraser but once she understood and saw the event for what it really was - which was the result of previous events - she realised that there was no need to be upset. Hence the suffering she felt went away.

In *The Luckiest Girl*, once the girls gave up their desires to be the most popular, the prettiest, the richest etc, they became free from those attachments and found happiness within.

Sometimes we are not only attached to desires. We can also be attached to bad emotions as well - for example our attachment to fear or stress which many of us find hard to resist. In *Examination Woes*, Uncle teaches Lily that her suffering (which takes the form of worry and stress) can be overcome through the practice of mindfulness. The next section: The Fourth Noble Truth tells us more.

THE FOURTH NOBLE TRUTH : THE TRUTH OF THE PATH

The Fourth Noble Truth tells us that there is a way - a path - that leads to the ending of suffering. This path is called the Noble Eightfold Path. It is very simply a guide to what you must do in order end suffering.

The Noble Eightfold Path consists of **Right View, Right Thought, Right Speech, Right Action, Right Livelihood, Right Effort, Right Mindfulness** and **Right Meditation**.

Right View means to have a correct view or understanding of yourself and of the world around you. A simple example of having the Right View is shown in the chapter *Oww That Hurt* where Lily stops feeling upset once she sees that there were reasons and occurrences that resulted in her incident with Evie. Lily realised she had to look at things in the right way - to have the Right View of things.

Right Thought means to think in the right way. In the chapter *The Race of Life* Mr Harold shows the children that when it comes to competing, there is no need to compare yourself with others. As he wisely said, when running a race, don't focus on others as you might get distracted. Run at your own pace and compare yourself with your previous performance, not someone else's because at the end of the day, your finish line is not at the same place as everyone else's. If you think carefully about it, everyone's life story is different. So why compare?

Right Speech is an easy one to understand but possibly not so easy to keep to! It simply means we should avoid lying, gossiping or saying things that will hurt others.

Right Action refers to what we do - our actions. We should not do things that can harm or destroy others such as fighting, killing, stealing and so on. And absolutely no violence!

Whatever jobs we do when we grow up or indeed whatever task or activity you do right now should follow **Right Livelihood**, meaning we should not live on work that would in some way harm or destroy others.

In everything we do, we should always do our best to become a better person. We should therefore always do things with the **Right Effort**.

Finally, **Right Mindfulness** means to be always aware and alert whereas **Right Meditation** means to have a calm and clear mind in order to see the true nature of things. In *Examination Woes*, Lily is so attached to her fear of failure that she lets emotion take over. However it is through Right Meditation where she calms down and her mind is no longer clouded by fear, that she sees the true nature of the problem and can then figure out how to overcome it. Right Meditation means the ability to see the true nature of things, including the ultimate nature of reality, which is: the past and the future are not real and that the present moment - Now - is all that is real and is all that we have. This is an important reason in practising Mindfulness - why regret the past or worry about the future when all you have to work with is the present moment - Now. Aren't Buddhists pragmatic?

Sometimes, even if we are aware of our fears, it is normal to be affected by this - we are human after all. One of the ways to tackle fear or stress is through the practice of Mindfulness - which means to be aware and to live in the present moment. In *Examination Woes*, archery was used as an example of how to do this. I had once read an article by Paul Coelho describing his love (obsession possibly!) for archery and how that allowed him to focus on the present. And so here, through archery, Lily learns to concentrate on the present moment, to focus and be aware of that very minute, to not worry about the past or the future, to embrace the tension and learn how to be in the world as it is.

So there you are - the four basic principles of Buddhist teachings. The first three Noble Truths are easily understood and you should be able to recognise and apply them in the things that happen to you and around you everyday. The Fourth Noble Truth is the part where we all need to practice (a bit like maths or reading really!) and is something we do daily. It is the stage where we make the genuine wish to be free from suffering through practice in developing our minds and our attitude to life. *It is the beginning of the Buddhist Path.*

https://tripitakaperusals.com
mld@tripitakaperusals.com

Dear reader,

If you've enjoyed this book, please leave me a review! I would love to know if Lily's misadventures have tickled your fancy, had you thinking or even made you cry!

You can also email me at mld@tripitakaperusals.com. I'd be interested to hear your feedback!

Check out https://tripitakaperusals.com to keep up with Lily's latest shenanigans, find out more about the next book, play games and win stuff!

Acknowledgements

I would like to thank the love of my life - my long suffering husband Jess (who is far more enlightened than I will ever be) - for his unwavering support and for not laughing in my face when I announced my search for enlightenment.

To my daughter Lily, from whom this book has sprung out of my love for her, and whose vivid accounts of her 'day at the office' provided me the impetus and invaluable source material for this book.

My mum, for her love, strength and no-nonsense view of life, Dad who will forever live on in my heart and in my stories, and to my aunt Valerie for her kindness, shining wisdom and for showing me the way.

I would also like to thank Helen Stables for her encouragement and advice, Mark Wicks for his meticulous proofreading whilst on holibobs in sunny Sorrento (sorry Mark), family and friends who have supported me in so many, many ways.

As the Theory of Emptiness goes, without any of the above, this book would not have come into existence!

M